COGNITIVE BEHAVIOUR THERAPY MADE SIMPLE

The Complete Guide to Overcome Depression, Worry, Anger, Anxiety and Negative Thoughts

Krystal Zhurov

Table of Contents

COGNITIVE BEHAVIOR THERAPY EXPLAINED?

Have you anytime thought about how your thoughts and emotions have affected your conduct? Or, on the other hand, whether thoughts and conduct are related? Is it possible that what you think intentionally or unwittingly can truly impact your life and even the lives of people around you?

Normally the problems that we face in our lives are a result of negative or faulty thought patterns that show themselves in our everyday practices, and we can't recall them. In this manner, we are trapped in the unending circle of negative thoughts inciting negative practices, which again causes negative thoughts. So how might we correct these faulty thought patterns and make life better? The suitable reaction lies in Cognitive Behavior Therapy.

Cognitive Behavior Therapy is a sort of psychotherapy that complements the importance of reasoning and how it impacts our emotions and actions. It relies upon the likelihood that our thoughts impact our actions, perspectives, sentiments, and emotions. Outside things like people, situations, and the earth are not the explanation behind our problems. If you correct your point of view and make a change in yourself, you can adjust better to comparative people and situations and limit yourself better in a comparative domain.

Cognitive Behavior Therapy is likely the most restricted sort of therapy open regarding time and successful results. A typical of 16 sessions or lesser is required depending upon the issue. The whole therapy process is sorted out and goal-arranged. The therapist and the client collaborate on the goal of the therapy and the decision to end the therapy when it has been accomplished. What makes it incredibly successful is the manner in which that each session has a goal that is picked by the therapist and the client. They have to deal with the methodologies in that session to land at a result and also proceed in each following session. In this manner, in each session, the therapist manages the client towards his goal by demonstrating his elective or better ways to deal with thinking and carrying on to achieve what they need.

Our practices and thoughts are discovered every now and again, so we need to unlearn the faulty thought patterns and relearn the correct thought and practices. The therapist teaches and aids in this procedure. At the point when the individual gets why and how he is getting along a particular activity, the sooner he can change it and increase capability with another activity. This can be a time-exhausting procedure. Thusly, we have a part uncommon to Cognitive Behavior Therapy, known as the Homework to speed it up. Close to the completion of each session, the therapist apportions the client to practice the methodology educated in the session and give some additional scrutinizing and exercises to be done. This helps to land at the goal faster.

Test verification has demonstrated this therapy to be compelling in problems going from Anxiety, Depression, Eating Disorders, Stress, Marital problems, Relationships, and so on. So Cognitive Behavior Therapy is a powerful therapy to deal with your problems with no other individual's information, make a change, and update the possibility of your life.

Cognitive Behavioral Therapy or CBT is a psychotherapeutic technique used by therapists to progress helpful change in people by watching out for their thought patterns, emotions, and conduct issues. Difficulties with unreasonable reasoning, broken thou by and faulty learning are recognized, and a while later treated using CBT. Therapy can be driven by people, social affairs, or families and the goals of CBT are to reconstruct one's thoughts, perceptions, and reactions, which support changes in practices.

The earliest type of CBT was developed by an American Psychologist, Albert Ellis (1913-2007), in 1955, naming his approach Rational Emotive Behavioral Therapy (REBT). Ellis (right) is looked on as 'the granddad of cognitive social medicines' Ellis credits Alfred Korzybski (who developed the speculation of general semantics, which accordingly impacted NLP) and his book 'Science and Sanity' for starting him in transit of building up REBT.

During the 1960s, an American Psychiatrist, Aaron T Beck, developed another CBT approach called 'cognitive therapy,' which was at first developed for depression in any case immediately transformed into a most cherished model to take a gander at considering the positive results it accomplished. CBT therapists acknowledge that clinical depression is commonly associated with conflictingly uneven thinking and senseless thoughts. CBT is at present used to give treatment in each and every psychological issue and additionally extends prescription consistency, understanding a prevalent result in broken behavior. A critical guide in CBT is the ABC system of senseless convictions; the three stages are:

An is the Activating event, the event that prompts a negative thought.

B is the Beliefs, the client's belief around the event.

C is the Consequence, the dysfunctional conduct that resulted from the thoughts and emotions starting from the event. A model would be: Susan is disturbed in light of the fact that she got a low imprint in her math's test, the Activating event An is that she bombarded her test, the Belief, B is that she ought to have decent evaluations, or she is futile, the Consequence C is that Susan feels discouraged. In the above model, the therapist would help Susan distinguish her irrational beliefs and challenge the negative thoughts dependent on the verification from her experience and afterward reframe it, which implies to re-interpret it in an increasingly sensible light. Another extremely significant guide in CBT is to empower a client to relate to the ten distorted thinking patterns:

1. All or nothing thinking - seeing things in dim or white, if your exhibition comes up short concerning great, you consider yourself to be a hard and fast disappointment.

2. Overgeneralization - considering a to be a negative event as a ceaseless pattern of annihilation.

3. Mental Filter - you choose a solitary negative annihilation and harp on it so as your vision of reality gets obscured.

4. Disqualifying the positive - you reject positive encounters by requesting that they 'don't tally,' keeping up a negative belief.

5. Jumping to determinations - you do a negative translation despite the fact that there are no unmistakable certainties that convincingly bolster your decision; this incorporates 'mind examining' and 'fortune-telling' or 'assuming.

6. Magnification (Catastrophising) minimization - overstating things or limiting things; this is moreover called the 'binocular stunt.'

7. Emotional thinking - assuming that your negative emotions mirror the manner in which things truly are, 'I feel making it, thusly, it must be substantial.'

8. Should make articulations - 'shoulds,' 'musts' and 'oughts' are guilty parties.

9. Labeling and mislabeling - rather than portraying your mistake, you annex a negative name to it, i.e., 'I'm a disappointment.'

10. Personalisation - you consider yourself to be the explanation behind some antagonistic outside event which, in certainty, you were not obligated for.

These are just a portion of the procedures utilized in CBT; others are relaxation techniques, communication skills training, confidence training, social skills training, and giving the client schoolwork assignments.

Pretty much, social cognitive therapy intends to assist a client with becoming aware of thought mutilations that are causing mental wretchedness and of individual conduct standards which are fortifying it and correcting them.

HOW CBT DIFFERS FROM COUNSELLING

Perhaps you are thinking about having some form of therapy; it can sometimes be difficult to choose which therapy is most appropriate to address your issues. The vast majority think about what counseling is, yet these days there are different alternatives, for instance, Cognitive Behavioral Therapy (CBT) and Neuro-Linguistic programming (NLP). I am a cognitive therapist giving NLP and CBT therapy in Hertfordshire. Regularly people get in touch with me to talk about how CBT and NLP, Hertfordshire shift from counseling therapy. This article will acquaint you with how these treatments contrast from customary counseling approaches.

Counseling includes meeting with a counselor and getting the opportunity to investigate by means of talking, difficulties you might be having, or distress you might be encountering. The counselors work to listen mindfully to what you are telling them to form a comprehension of your point of view of the difficulties you might be encountering. Counseling doesn't include offering guidance or dealing with a client to go in a specific direction. Through the process of being heard by a counselor, who is set up to reflect and assist you with clarifying your problem, counseling can be a method for engaging change, more choices, or of helping you discharge compelling emotion and feeling, which you have kept smothered or have felt incapable of imparting to family or companions.

During counseling, you can investigate and talk energetically about any part of your life, be it past, present, or later on, in a setting that is classified. Counselors acknowledge and respect their clients and provide a protected environment for the client to investigate their life, relationships, and themselves. Counseling can be valuable for helping people to oversee distressing emotions related to deprivation and misfortune. Counseling can be extremely helpful for you in the event that you trust you would profit by being listened to or feel troubled by inconveniences.

Cognitive approaches, for instance, CBT and NLP, are the two approaches used to advance positive change in people. Like counseling, the therapist will approach you with respect and provide a secret environment for you to work through your problems. Cognitive approaches are effective in facilitating emotional distress and conduct problems. In contrast to counseling, cognitive methods can be practiced by the individual and rely upon the perspective that the substance of our thoughts impacts our emotions and conduct. Through cognitive therapy, it is conceivable to learn approaches to destroy or deal with the sorts of thoughts you have, which equates to the fact that the state of mind they support, for instance, anxiety, can be settled. CBT and NLP are arrangement focused strategies that focus on the 'present time and place.' In contrast to other talking medications, for instance, counseling, the focus isn't on attempting to discover the origin of your distress (the therapist will take a full audit and inspect your past yet practical procedures to advance prosperity in the present is the principal focus) rather you will make sense of how to improve your state of mind at the present time. This includes acknowledging which elements keep up your distress or problem and learning techniques to conquer your problem, which you will practice voluntarily.

NLP is a scary name for what is a sound judgment, practical and effective therapy. 'Neuro' means cerebrum, 'phonetic' relates to how we use the language both to talk with others and inside our very own mind, and 'programming' relates to how we make and use patterns of conduct in regular day to day existence in order to get results. We understand that we experience the world through our faculties and that this information is converted into thoughts. How you utilize this internal language in your very own cerebrum straightforwardly influences your physiology, emotions, and conduct. People will, by and large, create propensities and patterns of utilizing internal language that have constructive or unfavorable consequences for their emotions and conduct. NLP therapy, Hert invigorates new points of view and choices in thinking, giving you more choices about your conduct and emotions, improving your communication and relationships, and creating suffering life skills.

Cognitive Behavioral Therapy focuses on how you consider a problem (cognitive) and what you do about it (conduct). CBT can tell you the best way to perceive and change faulty thinking patterns. This doesn't infer that you will consistently think positive thoughts. It is an approach to regulate running inauspicious thoughts, which feed anxiety and depression. CBT can assist you with comprehending overwhelming problems by separating them into plausible parts.

Both of these therapy strategies are practical and focused on problem illuminating in order to meet your therapy goals. This means not at all like counseling; sessions are increasingly sorted out and less free streaming as you move towards change with the assistance of your therapist. Regularly people will search for cognitive therapy, for instance, CBT Herts or NLP Herts, when they need answers for their problem or to move on from restricting thinking, emotions, or conduct.

Origins of CBT: Wilhelm Wundt is known to be the father of experimental psychology and established the first official research laboratory in psychology at the University of Leipzig; in fact, what was then considered experimental psychology is far from its current definition. It is also known that modern psychotherapy was born shortly afterward in Vienna, the effort of a certain Sigmund Freud. What is less recognized is that both experimental psychology and applied psychology have found fertile ground for its development in the United States. In fact, after Freud arrived in the United States in 1911, psychoanalysis swallowed up the field of psychiatry to such an extent that, within a few years, more than 95% of American psychiatrists had undergone psychoanalytic training. This monopoly of psychotherapy lasted until the late 1970s in the United States and until the 1980s in European psychiatric circles. In fact, the psychoanalytic crisis in terms of its ability to respond to changing social demands after World War II and "cure" had already escaped in the 1950s, coinciding with the birth of alternative psychotherapy models. Of these, behavioral therapy (BT) has certainly played a leading role.

Conducted in several parts of the world at the same time, thanks in part to the contribution of dissatisfied psychoanalytic therapists to its analysis and intervention instruments, BT has spread rapidly throughout Europe and has quickly established itself as one treatment that can provide effective solutions to patient suffering. Fifty years have passed since John B. Watson's pioneering work on behavioralism and cognitive-behavior in the introduction of the BT working model. However, the later evolution took place much faster. And the reason was simple: as with all models based on scientific thinking, BT was open to change, assimilation, and integration of ongoing research, not only in psychology but in other scientific fields, leading to new forms. Analysis and intervention. The first generation of BT, characterized by a radical change in well-established psychodynamic therapy, was quickly followed by a set of "innovations" that took into account previously neglected cognitive aspects. This fusion of behavioral & cognitive therapies is the origin of a second-generation BT called cognitive-behavioral therapy (CBT).

The Roots of Cognitive Behavioral Therapy: Going back, BT can be sub-divided into three generations. The first generation is part of a rebellion against the dominant therapeutic concepts of the time (psychoanalytic and humanistic approaches). The first interventions focused directly on reducing problematic behavioral manifestations using techniques based on well-defined and rigorously validated scientific principles. An example might be an individual suffering from social anxiety that avoids situations where he or she may be subject to judgment or criticism. The main goal of treatment would be to increase exposure to such social situations or to reduce anxiety resulting from stressful situations. However, BT was not immune to external events. The "cognitive revolution" in psychology began in the 1960s, and in the 1970s, many behavioral therapists influenced it by calling it cognitive-behavioral therapy (CBT).

Part of this movement argued that research was still relevant, but that the research that was supposed to influence second-generation behavioral therapy was research or a human student focused on cognitive pos; the argument was that it conditioned when people were not automated and direct. Rather, it is influenced by people's verbal and cognitive abilities. Mindfulness, attention, expectation, attributes, and linguistic representation were his terms that he felt were needed to publish learning. The argument was his model of conditioning animals unfavorable to study human learning because there are no unique human abilities, such as verbal skills. Therefore, following the model of

Preparing Animals, they must complement or replace the cognitive representations. As a result, the advent of cognitivism or the 1960s brought about paradigm shifts or kissing experimental psychology. Although the model has behaved the cognitive process as an epiphenomenon, a new approach seems to require or consider cognitive knowledge of paramount importance or psychological exploration, maintaining an empirical vision.

Cognitive therapy was born, and with it, the second generation of BT. The concept of associative learning is abandoned, giving way to more flexible principles that take into account the impacts of internal experiences (thoughts and feelings) in determining human behavior; Humans are mostly thinking beings, able to organize their behavior and modify it according to circumstances.

HOW CBT WORKS

The following features are big cognitive behavior interventions:

1. CBT is based on the emotional response behavioral model.

Cognitive behaviors therapy is based on the fact that our thoughts cause our behaviors and feelings, not external things, such as people, situations, and events. The advantage of this is that we can change the way we think we feel/act even if the situation does not change.

2. CBT is shorter and time-limited.

Cognitive behaviors therapy is considered one of the fastest in terms of outcomes. The average number of sessions clients receive (for all types of CBT problems and approaches) is only 16. Other forms of therapy, such as psychoanalysis, may take years. What makes CBT shorter is its very informative nature and the fact that it uses the task. CBT has a time limit because we help clients understand from the beginning of the therapy process that there will be a time when formal therapy will end. The end of formal therapy is a decision made by the therapist and for the client. Therefore, CBT is not an open and endless process.

3. A strong therapeutic relationship is needed for effective therapy, but not for the purpose. Some forms of therapy assume that the positive relationship between the therapist and the client is the main reason for improving the therapy. Cognitive- behaviors therapists believe that it is important to have a good relationship of trust, but that is not enough. CBT therapists believe that clients change because they learn to think differently and act in a consistent way. As a result, CBT therapists focus on teaching rational skills in self-mobilization.

4. CBT is a patient-therapist collaborative effort.

Cognitive- behaviors therapists seek to know what their clients want from life (their goals) and then help them achieve those goals. The work of the therapist is to listen, teach, and encourage, while the client's role is to express their concerns, learn, and implement this learning.

5. CBT is based on Stoic philosophy.

Not all CBT methods rely on stoicism. Stoicism is both reinforced by rational, emotional, behavioral therapy, and logical behavioral therapy. The behavioral therapy of Beck is not based on stoicism. Behavioral therapy doesn't specify what to do. More so, most people seeking therapy do not want what they feel. Techniques that emphasize stoicism teaches the benefits of feeling, in the worst case, calm when faced with undesirable situations. They have also considered that we are in undesirable situations, whether we are angry or not. If we are not satisfied with our problems, we have two problems: the problem and our discomfort. Most people want to have a few problems as possible. Therefore, when we learn to quietly accept a personal problem, we not only feel better but in general, we can better use our intelligence, knowledge, energy, and resources to solve the problem.

6. CBT uses the Socratic method.

Cognitive-behavioral therapists need a better understanding of the concerns of their clients. That's why they often ask questions. They also enjoin their clients to ask questions like "How do you know if these people are making fun of me?" "Can they laugh at something?"

7. CBT is structured and directive.

Cognitive- behaviors therapists have a specific agenda for each session. Specific techniques/concepts are taught in each session. CBT focuses on customer goals. We do not tell our customers what their "should" or "should" be tolerated. We are managers in which we show our customers how they think and behave to get what they want. As a result, CBT therapists do not tell their clients what to do but teach them how to do it.

8. CBT is based on an educational model.

CBT is based on the scientifically-based hypothesis that the most emotional and behavioral responses are learned. Therefore, the end goal of the therapy is to help clients perform their unwanted reactions and learn a new way of responding. However, CBT has nothing to do with "just talk." An added benefit is the emphasis on education by CBT:

it results in long-term outcomes. You know what to do to keep doing well as people understand how and why they are doing well.

9. The philosophy and methods of CBT are based on an inductive approach.

A key aspect of rational thinking is that it is based on facts. We often get angry over things when, in reality, the situation is not what we think. If we knew it, we wouldn't waste time bothering you. Therefore, the inductive method encourages us to consider our thoughts as hypotheses or hypotheses that can be questioned and tested. If we find out that our assumptions are wrong (because we have new information), then we can change our thinking to align ourselves to the real situation.

BENEFITS OF COGNITIVE BEHAVIORS THERAPY

Put patients under control.

Medication is often efficient by helping to suppress underlying emotions and thoughts so that the problem is never completely resolved. Cognitive-behavioral therapy, on the other hand, helps the patient identify negative thoughts and emotions, while the therapist helps them better understand how those thoughts and emotions control their actions. Then the patient can better master these thoughts and the resulting actions.

Absence of medication

Cognitive-behavioral therapy is conducted completely by speaking and acting. Although it can be used in combination with medicines, it can also be very effective in itself. In addition to not forcing the patient to take medication, this treatment can reduce the need for medication in a lot of patients over time, provided they consult their therapist regularly.

Effective treatment

Many patients do not know whether cognitive behavioral therapy will work or not, especially in Western cultures that have a greater emphasis on prescription drugs. Studies have shown that it can be effective in reducing the symptoms of multiple disorders, including anger management problems, depression, anxiety, social anxiety, post-traumatic stress disorder, sleep disorders, and many others.

Promote accountability

This form of treatment is based on a behavioral model, a model that says that a person's feelings control their thoughts and that their thoughts control their actions. Because of this, many people end up accepting responsibility for their actions instead of blaming others, situations or pretending to be because they are a victim. Although situations are often beyond the control of the person, their response to these situations is not, and one of the main beliefs that helped shape this form of treatment.

Long duration

Because medications do not solve the underlying problem, the patient often has to seek help for an occupational disorder for years. Cognitive-behavioral therapy, on the other hand, acts by changing the individual's mindset and helps replace negative thoughts with more positive thoughts.

For this reason, changes made when a patient undergoes cognitive behavioral therapy often lasts a lifetime, helping to reduce symptoms and ensure that they do not return.

Better relationships.

People often seek the help of an occupational therapist for addiction or other mental health disorders. This form of treatment helps reduce the annoying symptoms and, by doing so, makes the patient more self-aware than ever before. Just as patients can see how their thoughts affect their relationships and the impact of their actions throughout life, they can also see how their actions affect their relationships.

The end result is that many patients have better relationships in all aspects of their lives, including at work and at home, as treatment progresses and continues to progress.

This form of treatment continues to gain popularity as more and more people seek a permanent solution that medicines do not provide. It is also often referred to as "conversion therapy" because it basically involves talking between the patient and the therapist to discover the feelings and thoughts that control the actions. Speech therapy can help people with various mental disorders and many life difficulties and may reduce the need for medication over time.

Many studies show that CBT is an effective complement to the use of psychoactive drugs and medications to improve a patient's mental health. In fact, these studies also suggest that CBT may reduce the fall in mental health problems a patient may encounter. This adds to the fact that the symptoms of many of these diseases are also treated, reduced, and eliminated.

Some of the mental health problems that CBT can solve are:

1. Anxiety and panic: Many people have a disorder that causes extreme anxiety, panic, and an unpleasant feeling. These are also called anxiety attacks and panic attacks. CBT deals with emotions and thoughts about these disorders.

2. Obsessive-compulsive disorder: Also known as OCD, obsessive-compulsive disorder is a condition that causes the patient to adopt certain thinking and behavior habits. The most popular is the creation of obsessive thoughts and the obligation to take certain acts. CBT addresses these ideas and assists in finding solutions to these compulsive behaviors.

3. Posttraumatic stress disorder: Also known as a post-traumatic stress disorder, this disorder is caused by previous experiences of fear or traumatic stress. CBT aims to repair Thoughts that, in the present, contribute to dissatisfaction.

4. Phobias: There are many forms of phobias that are fears that are irrational and unfounded. Phobias are emotional, and CBT brings out the viewpoint of the client on these problems.

5. Depression: CBT deals directly with thoughts and depression. These thoughts, once addressed and corrected, can treat the symptoms associated with depression.

These are only a handful of other challenges CBT is able to address.

• involves very minimal risks

As a non-invasive method, cognitive behavioral therapy involves minimal risks. Even though CBT is a form commonly used with medication, the method itself has low risk. The steps associated with CBT do not cause physical harm. The methods involved in this type of therapy identify negative thoughts and seek to change them. These methods do not leave unanswered thoughts and represent a little risk to the patient.

Because it responds to negative fears and emotions, CBT can also cause temporary stress. Responding to fears and anxiety involves confrontation, which can cause distress to the patient. However, this is usually temporary because the solutions are followed immediately afterward. Examples of situations that can cause temporary distress include:

Exposure to phobias

Remember the experiences that led to post-traumatic stress disorder.

It addresses anxiety and panic.

Other situations that cause fear or distress.,

Patients are more aware of themselves and have a more positive outlook on life.

Many patients become more self-conscious after completing a comprehensive course of cognitive behaviors therapy. Self-awareness, in general, means more in tune with emotions, characteristics, and motivations. This is a positive trait since better self-awareness often leads to a better understanding of oneself. Greater understanding allows a person to be better prepared for stressful situations and appropriate reactions. This can help mitigate or prevent future problems.

Patients also gain a more positive view of life after CBT with the help of a qualified therapist. The main methods involved in CBT are to eliminate negative thoughts and to replace positive thoughts. This leads to the patient being more motivated to seek out negative thoughts and destructive actions and to actively replace positive thoughts.

List of the other effects of CBT on a person are:

Be more aware of potential stressors.

Learn how to solve it safely

You know how to stay away from stressors.

Being able to identify negative thoughts.

To avoid self-destructive actions.

I am more in line with mental health.

As a result, the positive effect of CBT goes far beyond what the patient achieves. This also leads to the patient having a generally more positive view of life.

Stress can have a negative impact on mental health.

• Its effectiveness has been proven by studies.

Various studies and scientific journals attest to the benefits of CBT. Many patients have improved, improved their mental health, and adopted a more positive attitude. CBT can also be practiced with other forms of therapy recommended by psychiatrists and therapists. It is effective only depending on the situation or can be used with other therapies to make positive changes faster.

Cognitive behavior therapy can lead to many positive changes in patients.

Many people believe that there is a penalty for treatment. There is nothing wrong with following treatment, especially if it is in the patient's interest. Consider the method of cognitive behavior therapy if you think you or a loved one need therapy. It has many benefits that go beyond issues of mental health.

OVERCOMING ANGER

What Is Anger?

Anger is an ordinary human emotion that everybody feels now and again. It can happen when you feel focused or when somebody encroaches on your privileges, undermines you, baffles you, or exploits you. It can run from inconvenience to uncontrolled anger. Anger can give you an eruption of vitality and push you to make positive changes in your life; however, it can likewise make problems in relationships and work.

There may be times that you feel your anger is advocated; somebody accomplished something incorrectly, and you reserve each option to be angry. Envision you returned home from work to discover your son playing video games. You had explicitly left directions for him to cut the grass, take out the refuse, and tidy up his room. None of this was done, and far and away more terrible, the kitchen is currently a wreck with his dishes from breakfast and lunch. He has clearly spent the whole day eating, sitting in front of the television, and playing video games. You are smoldering. At the point when a situation, for example, occurs, it is imperative to remember that while you cannot control the other person's actions, you can control your reaction. Sometimes anger bubbles up so rapidly you feel as though you have no control over it. Remember that you can control your reaction. Before exploding at your son, take a couple of moments to chill off and audit the situation. Ask yourself these inquiries:

- How important will this be in 60 minutes, tomorrow, one week from now, or one year from now?
- Is this value of being angry and destroying my whole night?
- What steps would I be able to take to resolve the situation?

You may decide that television and video games are killed until the chores are finished. You may decide that you will give your son another possibility tomorrow to finish the chores, yet make it clear that television and video games are beyond reach until the work is finished. You may take different benefits, for example, his wireless, away until he demonstrates he can adhere to your guidelines. You may decide later on he needs to content you photos of the finished chores before he is permitted to stare at the television or play video games. Posting the steps you can take causes you to feel back in control and can diminish the mind-boggling feelings of anger. In the event that this doesn't work, remove yourself from the situation by taking a walk, doing some activity, tuning in to some music, or getting a charge out of some action you find unwinding. When you have quieted down, take a gander at the situation again and think of steps to resolve it.

Healthy vs. Unhealthy Anger

Anger itself is neither healthy nor unhealthy. The recurrence, power, and articulation of your anger decide if it is productive or damaging. Healthy anger is milder, happens less regularly, and is used to take care of problems and set limits for yourself. It is communicated, talked about, worked through, and afterward let go. A few people experience difficulty controlling their anger, giving it a chance to bubble over and detonate. They use their anger to control, scare, control, or rebuff others. Unhealthy anger is out of the extent to the situation and normally keeps going longer than should be expected for the problem. Unhealthy anger happens more habitually than healthy anger. Visit, or extraordinary anger isn't healthy because it harms your safe frameworks, builds circulatory strain, and sets you up to be angry more than once. Search for a portion of these ways that unhealthy anger is imparted.

- Yelling
- Screaming
- Fighting
- Blaming
- Threats
- Violence
- Retaliating
- Holding hard feelings

- Ending relationships
- Punishing others

At the point when you express your anger in these ways, your needs may be met temporarily. Yet, you typically wind up distancing everyone around you or causing a struggle in your relationships. You may have legitimate problems because of battles or property decimation. When you quiet down, you may lament what you did or said; all things considered, when anger strikes once more, you react a similar way. Not communicating your anger is likewise unhealthy. You contain it inside, never telling anybody how you feel. Smothered anger has been related to hypertension, coronary illness, and malignant growth.

At the point when you deal with your anger in healthy ways, you use it as a manual to reveal to you something isn't right. It is your way of seeing frustration or treachery. Assume your youngsters are playing outside. A car speeds down the street. You blow up. "What's going on with that car? What a jolt! Don't they know there are kids playing? That is so dangerous!" You have a decision. You can react by pursuing the car, yelling, and waving your arms in spite of the fact that this most likely won't explain anything. You can make a positive move, engaging in your locale and working with the police to have signs and hindrances put on the street. You can use your anger to make a change. Communicating anger along these lines causes you to feel more in control of your life.

Common Hot Buttons

The term hot buttons are situations that trigger certain attitudes, which, thus, cause anger. While every person has hot buttons explicit to their life and past encounters, there are some basic topics that underlie a great many people's triggers. You can battle hot button triggers by utilizing coping statements, short affirmations that assist you with overseeing troublesome situations.

We should take a gander at certain instances of hot button triggers alongside the related attitudes and some recommended coping statements to help manage the situation.

Situation 1: Things don't go your way. Attitude: You feel entitled to your wants and become irritated when others prevent you from getting what you need.

Coping statements: "I have my needs and needs; however, others are entitled to differ or state no. I have to respect their entitlement to do that." "I have my needs, yet others have needs, as well." Example: You're ignored for advancement at work. Rather than thinking, "How could they; they double-crossed me," practice acknowledgment. "Everybody at work needs to excel. The person who got the advancement merits it as long as I do."

Situation 2: Something is unfair, or you are being exploited.

Attitude: You think everything ought to be fair, and if things are not simply, you feel the need to correct them.

Coping Statements: "I see fairness dependent on my perspective; others are entitled to their perspective." "Fairness is emotional. Others reserve an option to see things as per their own thoughts, standards, and desires." "Life isn't always fair; that is something I have to acknowledge." "Only one out of every odd fight merits battling."

Model: Your companion buys a costly accessory. You feel angry and envious and believe, "It's so unfair; I can scarcely pay my lease." Instead, practice acknowledgment. "Not everything in life is fair; I'm certain she has her fights, as well. It isn't for me to state how she ought to go through her cash."

Situation 3: Someone allows you to down or doesn't do what you anticipated.

Attitude: You assume others are purposefully attempting to hurt you or don't care about your needs.

Coping statements: "Nobody is great; not every person acts the way I would." "When somebody doesn't accomplish something that I expect, it doesn't mean they don't care about my needs. Others have their very own needs, and on occasion, they may contend with my needs."

Model: Your accomplice overlooks your birthday, and you assume it means he doesn't cherish you and is attempting to offend you. Rather, think: "I realize he isn't great about remembering get-togethers. I can assist him with excursion and remind him my birthday is approaching as opposed to setting him up to feel liable."

Situation 4: Others around you make similar slip-ups again and again. Attitude: You accept that you have to change them. You think if you make enough of an effort, shout at them, or grumble enough, you will eventually get them ready.

Coping statement: "Others have their very own strategies and cutoff points. Requesting they change without understanding their inspiration and impediments just prompts impasses."

Model: Your worker continues turning in his reports in a garbled way. You think, "What an uncouth bonehead; why is he so resistant?" Instead, have a go at thinking, "Evidently, he doesn't comprehend what I need in this report. I will plan a time for us to go over precisely how to finish these reports."

Reframe Your Emotion

Probably the most widely recognized problematic thinking processes in anger are personalization and marking. When you mark situations, others, or yourself utilizing extraordinary language, you can raise your anger and temperament. Practices, for example, reviling, calling others names, or misrepresenting the antagonism ("This is terrible!" "I have never been dealt with so inadequately!") makes the situation more regrettable as opposed to better. Rather than living in disbelief, attempt to acknowledge the situation. While experiencing a troublesome situation, record the elucidating words you use. Supplant the words with increasingly target or moderate depictions. Rehash your original statement utilizing the new words and check whether the degree of force of your emotion diminishes.

Original statement: "I can't accept he forgot my birthday! What a jolt! I am irate!" New statement: "He forgot my birthday. This is frustrating. I'm irritated."

Original statement: "I can't accept my doorman lost my package; what a nitwit! What a calamity. I am so disturbed. I have to report to him."

New statement: "My doorman lost my package. The conveyance framework isn't impeccable at my office. This is baffling. I have to call and document a case."

Accept Fallibility in Yourself and Others

You realize you are not an ideal person. You realize you make missteps, and you realize you have faults—you simply prefer not to consider them. You prefer to drive them to the back of your mind. All things considered, when you consider your faults, you should either think you are a horrendous person, or you should resolve to change. Disregarding your faults is a lot simpler. All things considered, you expect others to see and possess their faults. You expect them to assume liability for their slip-ups, and when they don't, you blow up. Incapacitating your anger begins with tolerating that you are fallible, alongside every other person. When you do this, you can see the triggers recorded in the past area from an alternate perspective. Suppose your accomplice overlooks your birthday. You are angry because he hasn't satisfied your hope. You assume that he is an impolite person and doesn't merit you. However, if you consider yourself to be fallible, at that point, the situation and your view of it changes. "He is forgetful; however, he gives me the amount he adores me in different ways. I have forgotten things previously and needed people to understand. I ought to understand when he is forgetful."

At the point when you are angry, you judge others. You see them as discourteous, rude, unfeeling, or unfair. You become angry because they are not carrying on the way you believe is fitting. For instance, suppose you are conversing with a coworker when another associate goes along and intrudes on the conversation. You think he is rude. What your attitude truly suggests is, "He ought to act the way I would." If you try to judge yourself first and remember that you hinder sometimes or do different things people dislike, at that point, you are increasingly able to see his behavior in an unexpected way. Remember, you can't compel anybody to change. You should change your behavior and your reaction.

Your Turn: Judge Yourself First

Attempt to find yourself setting a label on somebody. You most likely do this on multiple occasions for the duration of the day without thinking about it. Focus and tune in to how regularly you judge others. Stop and judge yourself. Spot a label on your reaction. For instance, when a colleague interferes with your conversation, you may compose that you are being eager. Perhaps he has a crisis or something important that should be talked about right away. This activity causes you to focus only on alone behavior instead of on others' behaviors.

OVERCOMING ANXIETY

Anxiety is a significant part of the time, confused with various feelings, especially dread. You may call anxiety "nerves" or "trepidation," anyway may be the primary information you have about the condition.

The word anxiety has been utilized since the 1500s and starts from the Latin word anxious, which means the stress of a dark event. Stress by then prompts a state of dread and powerlessness, which brings about both physical and mental effects. Notwithstanding the way that you probably won't know the qualification between anxiety and dread, the two terms suggest absolutely different feelings. Dread is commonly aimed at an external danger. The event you dread is identifiable. You may fear wandering off control when a vehicle is speeding by at sixty miles an hour or when a neighbor's pooch unexpectedly skips out at you. Anxiety has no such effectively obvious source and is consistently called an unexplained uneasiness. You may have a feeling of danger while experiencing anxiety; anyway, the feeling is vague, and at whatever point asked, you may state your feeling is related to "something dreadful happening" or "losing control."

Anxiety has physical, enthusiastic, mental, and even significant effects. Physical effects fuse quickness of breath, heart palpitations, trembling or shaking, sweating, smothering, nausea or stomach inconvenience, hot flashes or chills, wooziness, or instability. Since anxiety is so clumsy, you may change over your anxiety into anger or various feelings. Energetic effects fuse feelings, for instance, stress, anger, craze, and dread. Mental effects consolidate reasoning you're going to pass on, or that you're going crazy or are wild. Powerful effects fuse irritation and feeling separated and removed from yourself just as others.

You can all the more promptly grasp the possibility of anxiety by looking at what it is and what it isn't. For example, anxiety can be perceived from dread in a couple of various ways. Exactly when you are troubled, your dread is ordinarily coordinated toward some strong outside thing or situation. The event that you dread generally is inside the breaking points of credibility. You may fear not agreeing to a time requirement, shelling a test, being not capable deal with your tabs, or being expelled by someone you have to please. Exactly when you experience anxiety, on the other hand, you every now and again can't show what it is you're anxious about. The point of convergence of anxiety is more inside than outside. It is apparently a reaction to an indistinct, far away, or even unrecognized danger. You might be anxious when concerned about "losing control" of yourself or some situation. Or on the other hand, you may feel hazy anxiety about "something terrible happening." Anxiety influences your general existence. It is a physiological, social, and mental reaction simultaneously. On a physiological level, anxiety may join considerable reactions, for instance, brisk heartbeat, muscle pressure, queasiness, dry mouth, or sweating. On a social level, it can undermine your ability to act, convey, or deal with certain normal conditions. Rationally, anxiety is a dynamic state of dread and uneasiness. In its most uncommon structure, it can make you feel detached from yourself and even dreadful of passing on or going crazy.

Anxiety disorders

Anxiety is an expected and normal reaction to stress and can be beneficial in some situations. They can alert us to the dangers and help us be prepared and alert. Anxiety disorders vary from normal nervous or anxious symptoms and include intense fear or anxiety. Anxiety disorders are the most common mental disorders and affect almost 30% of adults at some point in their lives. But anxiety disorders are treatable, and there are several effective treatments available. Treatment helps most people lead a normal productive life.

Anxiety disorders are often associated with other mental health disorders, such as major depressive disorder, bipolar disorder, eating disorders, or certain personality disorders. This is also usually done with personality traits such as neuroticism. This observed occurrence is partly due to the genetic and environmental influences shared between these treatments and anxiety.

Anxiety disorders can guide people to try to avoid situations that trigger or aggravate their symptoms. Job performance It may likely impact school work and personal relationships.

In general, fear or anxiety is required for a person to be diagnosed with an anxiety disorder:

Being out of proportion to an inappropriate situation or age Prevents the ability to function normally. There are several types of anxiety disorders, including general anxiety disorder, panic disorder, phobia, agoraphobia, social anxiety disorder, and anxiety disorder with separation.

Causes of anxiety disorders.

The causes of anxiety disorders are not well understood. Life experiences like traumatic events appear to cause anxiety disorders in people who are already susceptible to anxiety. Inherited traits can also be a factor.

Medical causes

Anxiety can be correlated with an underlying health condition for some people. In some cases, anxiety symptoms and symptoms are the primary indicators of disease. If your doctor thinks that anxiety may have a medical cause, you can order tests to look for signs of a problem.

Examples of medical problems that may be related to anxiety:

- Illness of the heart
- Diabetes
- Thyroid problems, such as hyperthyroidism.
- Respiratory disorders, such as chronic obstructive pulmonary disease (COPD) and asthma.
- Drug abuse or withdrawal.
- Abandonment of alcohol, anti-anxiety drugs (benzodiazepines), or other drugs.
- chronic pain or irritable bowel syndrome

- Rare tumors that produce some fight or hormone leakage.
- Anxiety can sometimes be one of the side effects of some drugs.

Your anxiety may be due to an underlying medical condition if:

- You do not have a father (for example, a father or a brother) with an anxiety disorder.
- She did not have an anxiety disorder during her childhood.
- Avoid certain things or situations due to anxiety.
- You suddenly have anxiety that seems unrelated to your life events, and you have no history of anxiety.

<u>Risk factors</u>

These factors can increase the risk of developing an anxiety disorder:

- trauma Children who have been abused or traumatized or who have witnessed traumatic events have an increased risk of developing an anxiety disorder at some point in their lives. Adults who experience a traumatic event can also develop anxiety disorders.
- Stress due to illness. Having a health problem or serious illness can cause serious concerns about issues such as your treatment and your future.
- Accumulation of stress. A large-scale event or an accumulation of more stressful life situations can trigger excessive anxiety, for example, family death, work stress, or ongoing financial worries.
- Personality. People with certain types of personality are more likely than others to suffer from anxiety disorders.
- Other mental health disorders. People with other mental disorders, such as depression, often experience an anxiety disorder as well.
- Having blood relatives with an anxiety disorder. Anxiety disorders can occur in families.

Drugs or alcohol abuse or addiction to drugs or alcohol can cause or aggravate anxiety.

Types of anxiety disorders.

1. Generalized anxiety disorder
2. Obsessive-compulsive disorder (OCD)
3. Panic disorder

4. Posttraumatic stress disorder (PTSD)
5. Social phobia (or social anxiety disorder)

Generalized Anxiety Disorder (GAD)

GAD is the most widely known type of anxiety disorder. The main symptom of GAD is to worry about the diversity of activities and events. It may seem out of your control. You often feel anxious if you have GAD. You can feel "on edge" and attentive to the surroundings.

It can affect your daily life. You may find it affects your ability to work, travel, or leave home. You can also quickly get exhausted or have trouble going to sleep or focus. You may have physical symptoms, such as muscle tension and sweating.

If you have GAD, it is common for you to have other disorders, such as depression or other anxiety disorders.

GAD can be hard to diagnose, as it displays some of the specific signs of other anxiety disorders. Your doctor can tell you that you have GAD if you have been feeling anxious for more than six months, which has had a serious impact on your life.

Obsessive-compulsive disorder (OCD)

People with OCD may have symptoms of obsession, compression, or two. Such symptoms can affect all aspects of life, such as work, school, and personal relationships.

Obsessions are repeated thoughts, impulses, or mental images that cause anxiety. Common symptoms include:

- Themes of germs or contamination.
- Forbidden thoughts or unwanted taboos involving sex, religion, or prejudice
- Aggressive thoughts toward others or oneself.
- Have things symmetrical or in perfect order.

Complications are repetitive behaviors that a person with OCD feels the need to respond to obsessive thinking. Common compressions include:

Cleaning and/or excessive hand washing.

Order and organize things with precision and precision

Check things repeatedly, such as repeatedly checking if the door is closed or the oven is off consultative complete.

All rituals or customs are not compressions. Everyone sometimes checks things. But one person with OCD in general:

You cannot control thoughts or behaviors even when these thoughts or behaviors are recognized as excessive.

Use at least an hour a day on these thoughts or behaviors.

Do not experience the pleasure of behaving behaviors or rituals, but you may experience relief from the anxiety of thoughts.

You experience important problems in your daily life because of these thoughts or behaviors.

Some people with OCD also have a tick. Motor tactics are sudden, short, and repetitive movements, such as blinking of the eyes and other eye movements, facial grimaces, shrugging of the shoulders, and shaking of the head or shoulders. Compound community calls include repetitive sounds of scratching the throat, gardening or growing.

Symptoms can come and go, diminished over time or worse. People with OCD can try to help themselves by avoiding situations that cause obsession, or they can, To calm down, use alcohol or drugs. While most people with OCD know that their behaviors are unimportant, some adults and some children may not understand their behavior. OCT signs in children are generally recognized by parents or teachers.

Whether you think you have OCD, discuss your symptoms with your doctor.

Panic disorder

Panic disorder leads to regular panic attacks without a particular asset. It happens suddenly and feels intense and frightening. It is also possible to dissociate during panic attacks. You may also fear another panic attack.

Some situations can cause panic attacks, for example, if you don't like small spaces but need to use an elevator. This does not mean that you have a panic disorder.

Symptoms of panic disorder

Symptoms of panic disorder can include:

- an excessive sensation of terror or fear
- chest pain or sensation that your heart beats irregularly
- Feeling of dying or having a heart attack.
- Sweating and heatstroke or chills.
- dry mouth, shortness of breath or shortness of breath
- Nausea, dizziness, and weakness.
- numbness, tingling, or tingling in the fingers
- Need to go to the bathroom.
- a revolving belly
- Ringing in his ears

PTSD

Post-traumatic stress disorder (PTSD) is a disorder that develops in some people who have experienced a shocking, scary, or dangerous event.

It is natural to fear during and after a traumatic situation. Fear causes many changes in the body in a fraction of a second to help defend or prevent it. This "fight or flight" reaction is a typical reaction to protect a person from injury. Almost all have many reactions after the trauma, but most people heal early symptoms naturally. Those who continue to have problems can be diagnosed with PTSD. People with PTSD may feel stressed or afraid, even when they are not in danger.

Signs and symptoms

Although most, but not all, traumatized people have short-term symptoms, most do not develop continuous (chronic) PTSD. Not all people with PTSD have experienced a dangerous event. Some experiences, like a loved one's sudden and unexpected death, can also lead to PTSD. Symptoms usually begin early, within three months after the traumatic incident, but sometimes begin years later. Symptoms last longer than a month and are severe enough to interfere with work or relationships and be considered PTSD. The course of the disease varies. Some people recover within six months, while others have long-lasting effects. In some individuals, the disease becomes chronic.

A doctor with experience in treating people with mental illness, such as a psychiatrist or psychologist, can diagnose PTSD.

To be diagnosed with PTSD, an adult must have all of the following for at least one month:

At least one symptom of rebirth

- at least one symptom of avoidance
- at least two warning and reactive symptoms
- At least two cognitive symptoms and mood.
- Relieving symptoms include:
- Flashbacks - relives trauma over and over again, including physical symptoms such as heart attack or sweating.
- bad dream
- thoughts of fear
- Symptom recurrence can cause problems in a person's daily routine. Symptoms can begin with a person's thoughts and feelings. Words, objects, or situations reminiscent of the event may also initiate the recurrence of symptoms.

Social anxiety disorder or social phobia.

Many people are nervous or embarrassed, for example, Giving a speech or a new job interview. Yet syndrome of social anxiety, or social phobia, is more than shyness or nervousness at times. Social anxiety disorder is accompanied by an intense fear of certain social situations, especially situations that are unknown or where they feel monitored or evaluated by others. These situations can be so frightening that you are anxious to think about them or try to avoid them, which will disrupt your life.

The underlying social anxiety disorder is the fear of being examined, judged, or embarrassed in public. You may be afraid that people don't think well or that you don't feel good about others. And if you probably understand that your fears of being judged are at least a little irrational and exaggerated, you can't always help being anxious. But no matter how shy you are and no matter how severe the butterflies are, you can learn to feel comfortable in social situations and get your life back on track.

Causes social anxiety

Although you may feel that you are the only one with this problem, social anxiety is quite common. Many people struggle with these fears. But the situations that cause the symptoms of a Disorder of social anxiety may be different. EOLBREAK In most social situations, some people experience anxiety. Anxiety is associated with specific social circumstances for others, such as talking to strangers, interacting with crowds, or behaving in front of an audience. Common triggers for social anxiety include:

- Find new people
- have small discussions
- speak in public
- On stage
- be the center of attention
- be observed while doing something
- be mocked or criticized
- Talk to "important" people or authority figures
- be called to class
- Appointment
- Talk at the meeting
- Use public toilets
- Pass exams
- Eat or drink in public.
- Make calls
- Attending parties or other social gatherings.

Signs and symptoms of a social anxiety disorder.

Just because you sometimes get nervous in social situations doesn't mean you have a social anxiety disorder or social phobia. Many people feel shy or shy at times, but that doesn't stop their day-to-day functioning. Social anxiety disorder, on the other hand, interferes with your usual routine and causes extreme distress.

For example, it is quite normal to be nervous before giving a speech. But if you are anxious about society, you can worry weeks in advance, call a sick person to leave, or start shaking so much during the speech that you will be able to speak.

Signs Emotional signs and symptoms of a social anxiety disorder:

- Excessive self-awareness and anxiety in everyday social situations.
- The intense concern for days, weeks, or even months before a social situation arises.
- Extreme fear of being seen or judged by others, especially people who do not know.
- How to act in ways that embarrass or humiliate you.
- Afraid of others noticing that you are nervous
- Physical symptoms and symptoms:
- facc red or red
- Difficulty breathing

Stomach pain, nausea (butterflies)

- tremor or tremor (including trembling voice)
- Heartbeat or chest fatigue
- Sweating or heat stroke.
- dizzincss or weakness
- Behavioral symptoms and symptoms:
- Avoid social situations that limit your activities or disrupt your life.
- Be silent or mute to escape notification and shame.
- The need to always have a friend to go to
- Drink before social situations to calm your nerves

SYMPTOMS OF ANXIETY DISORDERS

Anxiety disorders can worsen, but with thc aid of a health professional, they can be controlled. The first line of action is to recognize the symptoms.

Here are some common symptoms of an anxiety disorder: the natural reduction of anxiety and the time to call a professional.

The muscles stretched

Having your muscles tense most days of the week is another common symptom of anxiety.

Tight muscles may be common, but we don't really understand why they are associated with anxiety.

It is possible that muscle tension increases the feeling of anxiety. Still, it is also possible that anxiety causes an increase in muscle tension or that a third factor causes it.

Interestingly, it has been shown that muscle tension treatment through muscle relaxation reduces anxiety in people with generalized anxiety disorders. Some studies also show that it is as effective as cognitive-behavioral therapy.

Panic attacks

A type of anxiety disorder called panic disorder is associated with repeated panic attacks.

Panic attacks produce an intense and excessive sense of fear that can be debilitating.

This extreme fear is usually accompanied by rapid heartbeat, sweating, tremor, shortness of breath, tiredness of the chest, nausea, and fear of dying or losing control.

Panic attacks can occur in isolation, but if they occur often and unexpectedly, they can be a sign of a panic disorder.

It is estimated that 22% of American adults will experience a panic attack in their lifetime, but only about 3% experience it often enough to meet the criteria for a panic disorder.

Sleep disorders are strongly associated with anxiety disorders.

The two most common problems are waking up in the middle of the night and having trouble sleeping.

Some studies suggest that having insomnia during childhood may also be linked to the development of anxiety later in life.

A study of nearly 1,000 children over the age of 20 found that childhood insomnia was linked to a 60% increased risk of developing an anxiety disorder at age 26.

Although insomnia and anxiety are closely related, it is not clear whether insomnia contributes to anxiety, whether anxiety contributes to insomnia or both.

It is known that when treating the underlying anxiety disorder, insomnia often improves as well.

Avoid social situations

You can show signs of social anxiety by:

Feel anxious or afraid of future social situations.

Concerned that others might judge or examine

Fear of being ashamed or humiliated in front of others

Avoid some social events because of these fears.

Social anxiety disorders are very common and affect approximately 12% of American adults at some point in their lives.

Social anxiety tends to grow early in life. In fact, about 50% are diagnosed before the age of 11, while 80% are diagnosed before the age of 20.

People with social anxiety may seem extremely shy and calm in groups or during new meetings. Although they do not seem anxious about the outside, they feel extreme fear and anxiety inside.

This distance may sometimes give the impression that people with social anxiety are presumptuous or distant, but this disorder is associated with low self-esteem, high self-criticism, and depression.

excessive worried

Excessive anxiety is one of the most common symptoms of an anxiety disorder.

Anxiety associated with anxiety disorders is disproportionate to events that trigger it and is usually found in response to normal everyday situations.

To be considered a sign of a generalized anxiety disorder, anxiety must occur almost daily for at least six months and be difficult to control.

The disorder must also be serious and intrusive, making it difficult to concentrate and perform daily tasks.

People under the age of 65 have the highest risk of suffering from a generalized anxiety disorder, especially single people, low socioeconomic status, and many life stressors.

Feeling Agitated

When a person feels anxious, a part of their sympathetic nervous system begins to sink.

This triggers a cascade of effects throughout the body, such as an accelerated pulse, sweaty hands, trembling hands, and dry mouth.

These symptoms occur because your brain thinks you have perceived danger and prepares your body to respond to the threat.

Your body will drain the blood from your digestive system to your muscles in case you need to run or fight. It also increases your heart rate and your senses.

Although these effects are useful in the event of a real threat, they can be debilitating if you are afraid of the head.

Some research also suggests that people with anxiety disorders cannot reduce their level of arousal as much as people without anxiety disorders, which means they can feel the effects of anxiety more. long time

Irritability

Most people with anxiety disorders also have excessive irritability.

According to a recent study of more than 6,000 adults, more than 90% of people with generalized anxiety disorder have an extremely irritable sensation during peak periods.

Compared to self-reported concerns, young and middle-aged adults with generalized anxiety disorder have reported more than twice as much irritability in their daily lives.

Since anxiety is associated with intense arousal and worry, it is not surprising that irritability is a common symptom.

Difficulty concentrating

Many people with anxiety say they have trouble concentrating.

A study of 157 children and adolescents with generalized anxiety disorders found that more than two-thirds had difficulty concentrating.

Another study of 175 adults with the same disorder found that almost 90% reported difficulty concentrating; the more serious the anxiety, the more problems it had.

Some studies show that anxiety can disrupt working memory, a type of memory responsible for keeping information short-term. This can help explain the dramatic decline in performance that people often experience during periods of high anxiety.

All the same, difficulty concentrating can also be a symptom of other medical conditions, such as attention deficit disorder or depression. Therefore, there is insufficient evidence to diagnose an anxiety disorder.

CBT THERAPY FOR ANXIETY AND DEPRESSION

What conditions can be treated with cognitive-behavioral therapy?

Cognitive behavior therapy is considered an effective treatment for the following disorders:

- depression
- Anxiety disorders (including social anxiety and generalized anxiety).
- Panic disorders
- bipolar disorder
- Personality disorders.
- eating disorders (including bulimia and bulimia)
- Abuse of psychoactive substances (such as smoke, alcohol, and other drugs)
- sleep disorders
- phobia
- obsessive-compulsive disorder
- Disorder with posttraumatic stress.
- CBT can also help to alleviate symptoms such as insomnia.
- relationship problems
- privacy concerns
- Nervous habits, such as skin scratches, contractions, and chase.
- chronic pain
- psychosis

What is cognitive-behavioral therapy?

In the first session, a cognitive-behavioral therapist works with the client to understand the individual's problems. Once the client's goals and priorities are clearly defined, the CBT therapist will develop a plan and give the client a treatment program. The therapist will also determine if the client is a good candidate for this type of treatment and ensure that he or she is comfortable with everything the treatment involves.

The first part of cognitive behavioral therapy is to identify thinking patterns and to assess their usefulness and validity. A person suffering from depression may constantly think they are not worth it, while a person suffering from a panic disorder may constantly think that they are in danger. These people really believe in their thoughts. As part of CBT, the therapist will question these thoughts and help the client understand his or her irrational beliefs.

The therapist may ask the client to consider these thoughts as hypotheses rather than facts, then the therapist and the client work together to test these hypotheses. If they prove to be false, they develop new ways of thinking.

Automatic thinking

Automatic thinking is an essential component of CBT. These are the immediate thoughts that enter a person's mind when an incident occurs that directly influence the emotional and behavioral responses to the incident.

A person's reaction to the sound of the window opening at night can be used to illustrate the concept of automatic thinking. Here are four different thoughts and automatic behaviors that can affect a person's reaction to the situation:

Person A assumes that the window is opened by an intruder who steals and kills it. Will be

Be afraid and try weapons or escape as soon as possible.

Person B automatically assumes that the child is at midnight. She is happy with the window opening and reacts enthusiastically.

Person C assumes that he is just his roommate, who often sits outside the house and forgets the keys. He was astonished and angry for his destroyed companion and later regretted it.

Person D believes aliens will come to take him to another planet. He feels frightened and powerless and might be paralyzed by fear in bed.

The situation is the same in all these examples. It is your interpretation that answers your answer.

Thinking Error

The automatic thinking of some people is unnecessarily negative, and they are not based on the reality of a situation; These are known as errors of thought.

The most common errors of thought are:

- Disqualify the positive: this involves constantly neglecting the good things that are happening or minimizing their meaning to maintain and reaffirm a negative belief.
- Overgeneralization: An individual takes the negative outcome of a single incident seriously and acts as if future incidents produce the same unpleasant outcome, even when there is evidence to the contrary.
- Mental filter: it involves emphasizing the negative aspects of a situation, however insignificant, and which inflates its importance. Everything that is good or positive is completely ruled out in favor of the negative.
- Think of everything or nothing: an individual sees each situation in black and white. Failure to win first place would be a complete failure, even if it came second. If a woman resists his advances, she must be ugly and destined to die alone.
- Personalization: This happens when a person believes that everything happens, even if it has nothing to do with the situation or has played a minor role.
- Unrealistic ideal: one person is constantly compared to another and always lacks precision because the latter generally has a specific advantage in the field in question. She makes an unfair comparison to her cost.
- Mind reading: This happens when one person believes that another person's actions are based on negative feelings about him or her. For example, to think that a friend did not return his call because he hates it, or to be convinced that the group of people speaking another neighboring language does not speak well about their appearance.

Automatic flows of negative thinking and habitual thinking error are not uncommon in people with disorders such as anxiety and depression. These people often have a negative view of the world, themselves, or the future.

Often, individuals are not aware of the automatic thoughts they make and, unconsciously, govern their behaviors. CBT helps people recognize and evaluate their automatic thoughts to understand why they have responded to a situation in the same way.

Afterward, CBT therapists help clients discover and challenge all kinds of wrong automatic thoughts or distortions that cause undesirable reactions to situations and begin the mission of replacing those failed automatic thoughts with more realistic thoughts. and more balanced This, in turn, leads to greater

the appropriate response is balanced in future interactions

The strategy involved in CBT

CBT generally involves many of the following strategies:

- Thought Record: People with TBI are often asked to keep a journal of thoughts in situations that inspire strong emotions. In some cases, the therapist will provide a worksheet with labeled columns that must be completed. Then, the client and the therapist review the worksheet together to look for trends in the person's thinking and to find ways to think and react in a healthier way.
- Behavioral experiences: These experiences help clients to check their perceptions and assess whether or not they are correct. e.g., a socially anxious woman who thinks everyone makes fun of her if she makes a mistake may have to voluntarily turn her purse on the subway. Not only does this allow you to see how many people are actually accomplished and how many people are accomplished are actually having fun, but it also allows you to see how much you can deal with this situation. This type of experience is used only after coping strategies have been implemented with potential consequences, and the client and therapist feel that the client is ready to try.
- Roleplay: Role exercises allow the therapist to demonstrate appropriate responses to difficult situations. The client and the therapist assume roles to give the client a realistic example of positive interactions. The consumer will change their behavior and adapt them to encounters in the future.
- Relaxation techniques: The therapist will teach the client some techniques that can be used to help relax in difficult or distressing situations. For example, you can demonstrate progressive muscle relaxation or guide the client through deep breathing exercises. Meditation is also sometimes used to help guests relax. The client should generally practice these techniques at home and then be

ready to use them to successfully deal with physical responses to disturbing situations, such as panic attacks, when they strike later.

- Assumptions test: This strategy demonstrates a person's beliefs about exceptions that make his "absolute rule" false. For example, a person who is convinced that he can never find a husband because he is boring and unpleasant may ask friends and family who seem to like his company or care about him. This shows that their belief is irrational and gives them a starting point for a more balanced belief; She can see the evidence that she is really friendly and funny and begins to think that it may not be impossible to find a partner later.

Additional components can be used depending on the specific problem being addressed. For example, exposure therapy could be used as part of CBT for people with specific phobias. Since the event that fears can often reinforce, the idea is to expose the client to something that raises their fear to help them overcome. Therefore, a person who is afraid of papaya may be gradually exposed to it over a period of time, which increases the level of exposure to help the client develop sensitivity to spiders until his animation has no longer damaged a reaction of fear or panic.

Benefits of cognitive behaviors therapy

It works in a relatively short period of time.

Teach clients the skills they can use to control their thoughts and behaviors in daily life, even after the end of treatment.

As a drug, it can be effective in treating other disorders.

It is a flexible therapy that can be tailored to the individual needs of each individual.

This helps people learn to see situations realistically, to cause less negative feelings than their previous thinking habits.

It is based on the objects of the customers.

You can also use It to help a variety of people, Irrespective of their language, faith, gender, age, or socioeconomic status. It is based on the universal laws of human behavior and is therefore suitable for many people.

What is the effectiveness of cognitive-behavioral therapy?

The effectiveness of CBT in treating various disorders has been demonstrated by hundreds of clinical trials. It is considered to be one of the most effective anxiety and/or depression treatments.

CBT's efficacy can be attributed to the following features:

- Focuses on goals and problems.
- Teach clients strategies and skills that have proven effective.
- It is highly structured.
- Stresses a strong relationship between client and therapist.

How Long Does CBT Work?

A typical course of cognitive-behavioral therapy will include weekly sessions over a period of about two months. However, the exact number of sessions may vary depending on the individual. While some people feel better after only six weeks, others may continue treatment for six months or longer.

Some people may choose to attend maintenance sessions several times a year or every two years after the end of initial treatment to make sure they are right and to resolve any new problems. Many feel that they have learned the skills they have gained and are able to apply them in a way that will no longer require future visits.

Some of the factors that influence the duration of treatment are:

The individual needs of the client.

How long has the problem been?

The severity of the problems found.

Frequency of sessions.

The duration of each session.

Progress made by the client outside the therapist's office.

Challenges and limitations of cognitive-behavioral therapy

Although many people successfully deal with a variety of psychological problems with cognitive behavioral therapy, this type of therapy is not suitable for everyone and does not work in all cases.

The challenges and potential limitations of CBT include:

- The client must do some work. The therapist acts a bit like a personal trainer could act in a gym; She will advise and encourage the client, but she must be ready to do her part to get results. This approach is not suitable for everyone, and some people may prefer other psychotherapies with a more flexible structure.
- Does not work overnight. Cognitive-behavioral therapy generally requires a constant commitment to regular appointments over a few months. It generally works quickly, but those who expect immediate results are discouraged.
- This requires some motivation from the client. Attending regular sessions and doing the necessary work requires some client motivation, which is a problem for many depressives. Therapists are ready to face it, but the client must show their willingness to see the results. For some people, it may seem like it is in a hurry and therefore is not the best approach. Other approaches to psychotherapy, which have a more flexible structure, may seem more appropriate for these clients.
- There can be difficult times. In general, CBT is based on a positive relationship between the therapist and the client. However, A person can leave their comfort zone to face problems like phobia or anxiety. This is always achieved in a controlled manner with the end goal of helping to solve the problem.

How does it compare to alternative treatments?

Cognitive-behavioral therapy compares favorably with other treatments for anxiety and depression, such as medications and other forms of psychotherapy.

Some studies have shown that CBT is as effective as antidepressants for certain types of depression and seems to work better than medicines to prevent Depression relapse. It can also be used in conjunction with medicine to increase the chances of successful treatment and to provide coping mechanisms for clients that can be used during treatment roasting.

Since CBT is primarily concerned with "here and now," people with problems that include a component that is also connected to life experiences may have better outcomes than other approaches to psychotherapy.

How cognitive behavioral therapy works

Cognitive-behavioral therapy, or CBT, is a method for short-term therapy that can help people find new forms of action by modifying their style of thought.

Becoming involved with CBT can help people reduce stress, deal with complex relationships, deal with pain, and face many other life challenges.

CBT is based on the fact that the way we think and interpret the events of life has an impact on our behavior and ultimately on our feelings. Research has shown that in certain cases, it is useful.

More specifically, CBT is a focus on specific goals and problems that requires the active participation of the individual to succeed. Focus on your current challenges, thoughts, and behaviors.

It is also limited in time, which means that the person knows when a course will end and knows something about what to expect. Often, a class includes 20 individual sessions, but this is not always the case.

It can also take the form of an individual or group session.

CBT is a collaborative therapy that requires the person and the counselor to work together. According to the American Psychological Association (APA), people stop learning to become their own therapist.

CBT can help fight depression, anxiety, and a number of other issues.

CBT is a psychotherapy form that focuses on how the thoughts, beliefs, and attitudes of a person affect their feelings and behavior.

The APA notes that CBT is based on a number of beliefs, including:

Useless ways that people think can lead to psychological problems.

If people learn to behave unnecessarily, it can also lead to psychological problems.

People can learn new ways to think and act.

New habits can alleviate the symptoms of mental and physical disorders and allow people to act better.

Practitioners based CBT on the idea that problems arise from the significance people attach to both events and things themselves. Unnecessary Thought can make it hard for a person to work in different situations with trust.

CBT can contribute a positive impact on how people feel and behave and provide training strategies to help them deal with challenges.

Research shows that CBT can support people with depression, panic disorder, and other health problems. There is also increasing evidence that it can help alleviate chronic pain.

CBT is a broad concept. Different types of CBT focus on different aspects of life. Some types deal with specific issues, such as emotional or social issues.

A CBT course is a series of sessions in which an advisor and an individual or group meet regularly and collaborate.

What Can CBT Treat?

Therapists created the first CBT models about 50 years ago. A reliable source for treating depression. There is

Now models for dealing with a wide range of conditions, including:

- Panic disorder
- PTSD (PTSD)
- generalized anxiety disorder (GAD)
- marital conflict
- social phobia
- childhood depression
- anger
- insomnia
- Dependence and addiction

- eating disorders
- many other mental and physical conditions
- Borderline personality
- Dental phobia
- Research has shown that CBT can reduce the symptoms of health problems that some treatments cannot reduce.

How it works

In order to better understand current feelings, some forms of psychotherapy focus on the past. CBT, on the other hand, focuses on existing beliefs and principles.

CBT can help people with many things that are important to thoughts and beliefs. This stresses the need to recognize, question, and change the perception of a person's situation. EOLBREAK According to the CBT, people's thinking is to put on a pair of glasses that allow us to see the world in a specific way. CBT makes us more aware of how these thinking patterns create our reality and determine our behavior.

Change distortions and perceptions.

CBT can help people find new ways to see things.

CBT aims to transform every way of thinking and acting that avoids positive results. For example, when a person suffers from depression, their perceptions and interpretations are misplaced.

A distorted view can make a person more likely to:

a negative mental state

have come to a conclusion

view catastrophic situations incorrectly

see things as good or bad with nothing in between

When people learn to be scared or pessimistic, they will automatically start worrying about it. CBT's aim is to question these automatic thoughts and equate them along with reality.

If a person can adjust their way of thinking, their anxiety is reduced, and they can function in ways that benefit and those around them.

As individuals acquire new skills, they find it easier to solve problems constructively. This can reduce stress, help them feel more in control, and reduce the risk of negative mood.

An example: dental phobia

A person with dental phobia, for example, is afraid to go to the dentist because he thinks he will suffer severe pain, even death When the dental operation is underway. With a negative experience in a previous time, perhaps in childhood, this fear may have started.

A CBT therapist can collaborate with the person to correct the wrong thought that says, "Because I have pain with a filling, all visits to the dentist will be painful."

Together, the client and therapist can develop a plan to view dental treatment in a new way and overcome fear.

CBT is a kind of psychotherapy where a person learns to change their perceptions and how they see things in their lives. This can affect behavior and attitude positively.

CBT can help people with many problems, from depression to chronic pain.

An advisor and a client work together to identify goals and expected outcomes. To take advantage of it, the person has to be an active participant.

Anyone considering taking a CBT should find a qualified professional. A doctor may advise CBT specialists on the spot.

Counseling and therapy may be costly, but there are also self-help classes available.

In 2012, some researchers said that an online self-help program for CBT was beneficial for people with chronic back pain. This could be a profitable option for some people in the future.

Effective treatments for anxiety.

Several studies have shown that two types of treatment reduce the symptoms of anxiety disorders: (a) certain types of medication and (b) certain types of psychological treatment called cognitive-behavioral therapy (CBT), for short). This section briefly talks about the pros and cons of each type of treatment and then focuses on CBT, which is our specialty in ASDC.

Anxiety medicines: advantages and disadvantages.

The main categories of drugs that have been widely researched and understood to be effective in reducing the symptoms of anxiety disorders are selective serotonin reuptake inhibitors (SSRIs, for example, Paxil), tricyclic antidepressants (e.g., Anafranil Example), monoamine oxidase inhibitors (MAOI); Nardil) and benzodiazepine (e.g., Klonopin).

The benefits of using drugs to treat anxiety disorders include:

They are often effective: up to 50% of people who use these medications experience at least symptom relief.

They are easy to get: a doctor (often a psychiatrist) prescribes them, and the medicine is widely available.

They are easy to use: the pill does all the work in your body.

The disadvantages of using anti-anxiety medications are:

Not everyone responds well: 50% of people taking these medications do not respond.

The reduction of symptoms is generally moderate: the average rate of improvement is between 20% and 40%.

Side effects are common, although they are usually moderate and can be managed quite well.

You should continue to take the medication over the long term; Generally, the symptoms reappear if the medication is discontinued.

CBT Treatment for Anxiety: Advantages and Disadvantages

CBT is a set of psychological treatment strategies that consider the patient/client as an active participant in their treatment. It is considered beneficial for the patient to understand exactly what the treatment involves and the ideas that underpin the use of these treatment techniques. The techniques used in CBT were tested with thousands of people with anxiety issues in hundreds of studies. These studies ' results show that CBT is often very effective in reducing anxiety and related issues. A complete CBT description is provided below.

The benefits of CBT to treat anxiety are:

This is an effective short-term treatment: Research indicates that more than 60% of people with CBT experience a substantial improvement in their anxiety symptoms.

It's the best long-term treatment: CBT teaches you skills that no one can take away.

CBT is brief: In general, a significant improvement is achieved in 12 to 20 treatment sessions.

The disadvantages of CBT include:

It's hard work: CBT requires you to learn and exercise new skills that can be difficult.

Addressing Your Fears: One of the elements of most CBT interventions is to gradually address the situations that cause anxiety. This means that you probably feel anxiety as a "side effect" of the treatment.

It is difficult to find experienced therapists: relatively few psychotherapists have the training and experience to qualify as experts in TBI.

What can you expect from an anxiety problem if you have an LCT?

CBT is based on the reasoning that anxiety disorders involve behavior and a pattern of maladaptive thinking. Anxiety-related thinking patterns generally include the tendency to overestimate the likelihood and severity of the negative consequences. That sort of thinking contributes to panic feelings and other strategies to reduce anxiety ("safety behaviors"). These behaviors serve to escape anxiety situations, but they also prevent the person from discovering that these situations are not as dangerous as he thought. As a result, the person crashes while performing wrong behaviors that keep their fears alive. As part of CBT, people learn new ways of thinking and behaving in situations that create anxiety so that they realize that such situations are not dangerous.

The first step in CBT is to get a complete history of staff experiences and psychological functioning and to assess whether a medical or psychiatric consultation is necessary. A medical consultation is often helpful to rule out possible physical / medical causes of anxiety symptoms, and psychiatric consultation, although occasionally scheduled, is particularly important for people who are weaker from anxiety symptoms that they cannot cope with. . Failure to follow treatment. Effectively with less help from drugs.

Afterward, the person will discover the nature and experience of the anxiety and their particular anxiety problem. This involves learning to better observe, record, and report the causes, thoughts, feelings, and behaviors related to anxiety. All of this helps the therapist better understand the person's specific anxiety problems. The better we understand how a patient has an anxiety disorder, the better we can design an effective cognitive-behavioral intervention. Then a "road map" of the person's symptoms develops. A care plan outlining the basic patterns of thought and actions to be modified during therapy and the strategies to be used.

Cognitive restructuring is a strategy for identifying and coping with styles of maladaptive thinking that fuel anxiety. In essence, you have to learn to ask yourself, "What do I say about this situation that makes me so anxious?" Once these thoughts are identified, the person will learn to critically analyze the validity of these ideas and develop a new one. Set of reflections based on a more rational (evidence-based) approach

situation assessment The difference in the power of positive thinking, which is essential to tell a person what is right, "cognitive restructuring is based on the power of logical or critical thinking, as with all abilities. Develop in CBT Cognitive restructuring Learn during treatment sessions and practice the same patient.

The next step in CBT is usually one or more variations of the therapeutic exposure where the person exercises against their fears. Therapeutic exposure (instead of daily exposure of some people) is done carefully and under the direction of a therapist. It is generally progressive, which means that exposure begins with the resolution of easier situations and then with the development of more difficult situations. The person also performs self-report exposure work between treatment sessions.

Although exposure therapy may seem difficult, you are well prepared to address these issues when you fully understand the problem and the techniques of cognitive restructuring. By developing a hierarchy or a list of fears, the patient gradually challenges himself, starting with less difficult topics, developing strength and self-confidence, advancing into more fearful ascending situations. Long-term maintenance of gains, prevention of relapses, and "late response protocols" or ways to treat symptoms that may return.

As you can see from the procedure described above, the treatment focuses on reducing, if not eliminating, the symptoms of anxiety. However, in addition, throughout therapy, additional problems are often addressed. If the initial assessment reveals specific trauma problems or family history, these problems can be incorporated into CBT. Comorbidity may exist as separate problems but often linked to anxiety, most commonly depression and/or substance abuse. These conditions and other comorbidities can also be addressed in treatment if necessary. Problems related to self-esteem and interpersonal functioning are almost always addressed as part of the treatment. The development and/or improvement of out-of-support systems is encouraged. Finally, respect, support, and stimulation in the therapeutic relationship are essential to the success of the treatment.

HOW CBT TREATMENT FOR CONTROL OF ANGER, DEPRESSION AND ANXIETY

CBT for panic attacks

This happened again. One minute, I was trying to fall asleep, and the next thing you knew was that you were in bed, trying to breathe. You started walking, you opened a window, you sat and sat down, but nothing seemed to help. As your heartbeat fast, your anxiety grew to the point that you were wondering if it was the end for you. However, about 20 minutes later, you were still alive and could see the incident for what it really was: another panic attack.

There are a few things in life that are scarier than a panic attack. This may be something you can remove if it occurs once or twice, but if you suffer from regular panic attacks, you need to find a good solution so that you can take control of your life and not be scared of the next attack. This happens one of the ways in which many people may be facing panic attacks is through cognitive behavioral therapy.

What is a panic attack?

A panic attack is a sharp increase in intense symptoms, including:

- physical symptoms
- heart palpitations
- perspiration
- shake or shake
- chest pain
- If you are tired or tired.
- hot or hot shots
- mental symptoms
- An abrupt increase in anxiety, whether or not it is caused.
- Feel separate from your surroundings
- Intense fear of becoming sick or dying.

The attack can be caused by a specific or unexpected situation and generally lasts between five and twenty minutes.

During a panic attack, your mind perceives a threat that causes your body to enter into combat or flight. Your body is trying to absorb more oxygen, which can cause rapid and fast breathing. In addition, hormones such as adrenaline are released, resulting in rapid heart rate.

Panic attacks are very scary when they occur, and although they are generally not harmful to health, some people say they feel dead when they are in a panic attack. As a result, some people are afraid to leave home for fear of public attack.

How Can CBT Help With Panic Attacks?

Cognitive-behavioral therapy, or CBT, is a type of treatment that examines the relationships between thoughts, feelings, and behaviors and helps people discover certain ways of thinking that lead to destructive beliefs or actions.

CBT does not consist of endless hours lying on a couch and talking about your childhood with a therapist. Instead, it is goal-oriented therapy that focuses on a specific problem. It is also an active intervention since patients must practice the skills learned outside the therapist's office.

Although panic attacks are physically apparent, they are primarily a psychological problem, and finding the basis is the best way to control panic attacks. A CBT therapist can examine patterns of thinking that trigger or support a panic attack and help patients rethink their fears and anxiety more realistically.

Treatment of panic attacks with cognitive behavioral therapy generally involves a sincere assessment of the following components:

Your thoughts lead to a panic attack.

How do you react when an attack happens?

The thoughts that cross your mind during the attack itself

Your therapist will help you replace negative thinking patterns with more balanced models that won't pose to trigger panic attacks.

Much of its success as a treatment for panic attacks is in the fact that CBT allows people to acquire useful thinking management skills that can be applied to everyday situations. Your therapist may also suggest breathing techniques and other mitigation mechanisms relieve symptoms when you have a panic attack.

How effective CBT is in the treatment of panic attacks

CBT is considered one of the most effective psychological treatments for panic attacks. Even though no treatment works for everyone, its high success rate makes it an excellent starting point for most people. For an average of four months, the National Institute for Health and Care Excellence (NICE) suggests 7 to 14 hours of CBT, but the Therapist may suggest a time scale appropriate to the severity of your problem.

Try to remember the next time a panic attack occurs that you are not in danger and that particular feeling is going to pass. Consult a therapist who specializes in cognitive behavioral therapy if you want to minimize the frequency and severity of future panic attacks.

How CBT therapy can help treat phobias

Cognitive-behavioral therapy of phobia

Some issues are natural and unreasonable, but others seem excessive against the level of danger presented. Such fears cause unnecessary pain and distress. They can undermine self-confidence, block pleasure, and prevent you from doing things you may or may want to do.

If you are afraid or intensely afraid of certain situations or things, you may be suffering from a phobia.

Cognitive-behavioral therapy is a particularly effective treatment for people who want to treat phobias.

How can CBT therapy for phobias help?

During and after a successful CBT therapy course for phobias, you can expect to experience some of the following:

Discover new insights and perspectives that will help you understand why the phobia provokes intense fear reactions in you.

Find out how certain ways of thinking and behavior keep you phobic and how they can be resolved.

Learn how different ways of thinking and behavior can reduce the intensity of your physiological response

for phobia, it calms your fears and allows you to deal with the situation more confidently

Learn how to completely manage or suppress your reaction to the phobia

Being able to engage in a previous phobia with confidence, without worrying about debilitating issues.

Meaning of phobia

Phobia is a kind of anxiety disorder that involves an irrational or excessive fear of something or the situation. People suffering from a phobia are suddenly struck by a deep fear of the idea of finding the phobia actuator.

Symptoms of phobia

You can encounter one or more of them if you have a phobia. of the following symptoms when you come in contact with an object or situation you fear:

- Anxiety
- Panic
- rapid heart rate or breathing
- perspiration
- chest pain
- tremor
- Dizziness
- depression

From a diagnostic point of view, to qualify as a phobia, the fear you feel needs to be out of proportion to the reality of the triggering situation.

Common phobia

While people can develop a phobia of almost anything, some phobias are more common than others. Here is an example of some common phobias and the impact on people:

- Social anxiety disorder: It is anxiety for the opinions and judgment of others. This can save you from interacting with people, especially strangers, for fear of acting ashamed or not being loved by people.
- Claustrophobia: Fear of being trapped or simply entering a confined space. This can prevent people from taking the elevator, taking a train or train, or not leaving them completely.
- Agoraphobia: Fear of crowded spaces and is often fueled by the worry of not being able to escape if something happens. Victims may be afraid to enter stores, cinemas, restaurants, sporting events, or public transportation, and people are often confined to their homes.
- Fear of flying: Fear of traveling by plane, helicopter, or other flying objects. This can limit movements to the point of damaging family relationships when traveling on vacation or raising professional problems when work trips require flying.
- Dental issues: A dental phobia can encourage people to avoid receiving proper dental care, exposing them to the risk of gum disease and other dental problems related to serious health problems, such as heart attacks. And the shot.

Cognitive Behavioral Therapy Treatment of phobia

CBT treatment is voice therapy that shows how certain patterns and cycles of thought and behavior can affect our healthy functioning.

Through a process of research, psychoeducation, and written exercises, a CBT therapist will help you understand the types of thoughts and patterns of behavior in which you can participate, which facilitate or exacerbate phobia. Then, through a series of additional exercises and experiments, your cognitive-behavioral therapist will assist you in discovering another perspective and more effective strategies to completely reduce, control and/or eliminate the phobia and fears associated with your life.

A CBT therapist can also help you discover certain behaviors that ease and aggravate the phobia. For example, many people with phobias do their best to avoid exposure to the things they fear, and exposure therapy can be a part of the behavioral component of treatment. This may involve gradual exposure to the trigger, which increases with time so that it no longer ignites a panic reaction.

CBT therapy for phobias is the most reliable and effective if you can actively participate in the task. These may include keeping a journal, performing a reflection exercise, or trying out a new behavioral strategy.

How much do CBT phobias need to be overcome?

In general, weekly CBT sessions of approximately one hour over several weeks may be sufficient to overcome the phobia. If other problems that also affect your psychological well-being, such as anxiety or generalized depression, may take a little longer to achieve the desired result.

DEPRESSION

At the point when buried in depression, joy escapes you. Joy is mysteriously absent; your ambitions clot. Your strength tends to leaves you. You worry. You lose your confidence. You think you are hard to love. Your thoughts fill with cries of helplessness and hopelessness. You feel trapped. Your attention is adrift. You try to vanish. Your relationships sharp. You feel stuck, desensitized, dull, lifeless. Paradoxically, you may feel irritable and furious. Encapsulated within a persistently negative mood, gloom appears to be impenetrable. Interests are clammy ended. This process practically always includes patterns of negative, burdensome thoughts, including helplessness, hopelessness, and worthlessness. What is the reason for depression?

Here is depression's point of view: "I am depressed. Cold like an arctic mist, I hose your spirit and your spirit. I fill your thoughts with gloom. At the point when I am with you, you are but a withered leaf beneath wet snow with no place to go. Still, I can do much more. I can fill your mind with cemetery thoughts and make you teary. I can cause you to complain and bicker. I can make you feel uncertain. I can drain all supplication sure from your life. I can drive chuckle into the shadows. I can delve you into a gap so profound that you can't see the top. I can then overwhelm you with thoughts of helplessness and hopelessness, so you won't try to get out, for I am in the mood of depression. Only I can control what you do and feel."

This description of depression may sound a bit dramatic. Nevertheless, you'll find a tone of desperation in depression that you can't disregard. Like a destructive tenant, depression once in a while forgets about with strong encouragement.

Depression is an ordinary period of living for millions. Bitterness, bereavement, feeling down, and feeling depressed are all part of the human condition. Practically everybody will, over their lifetime, experience some level of depression, some much more so than others. Depression comes with a kind of melancholic mood that is customarily weighted with negative thinking. It normally follows extraordinary stress, but for a few, depression (and maintaining a strategic distance from depression) is a way of life. Yet depression isn't in charge of your life. Although depression can feel desensitizing, this mood is vulnerable. As you detect and expose droning depressive thoughts and participate in anti-depressive behaviors, depression tends to lift. There is sound motivation to be optimistic that you can get help from depression.

Types of depression

1. Major Depression

This is the most commonly known kind of depression. It is additionally alluded to as Major Depressive Disorder. It tends to be caused due to any major event or even a progression of littler events or problems. A person is determined to have major depression if he/she shows symptoms of depression (given beneath types) for more than about fourteen days.

2. Constant Depressive Disorder

In the event that a person has experienced depression for over a time of 2 years, it is called an industrious burdensome disorder. In spite of the fact that the cause of depression might be the same as major depression, for reasons unknown, the person might be unequipped for defeating it. Already PDD was known as dysthymia.

3. Manic Depression

Manic depression is all the more commonly known as Bipolar Disorder. On account of bipolar disorder, a person encounters extraordinary emotional episodes, extending from inconceivable highs to burdensome lows. The person can't control his behavior and may make radical strides.

Manic depression is one of the most genuine forms of depression.

4. Seasonal Affective Disorder

It is a form of depression that is seasonal in nature; for the most part, it occurs during the winters. People who have seasonal depression think that it’s hard to adapt in the absence of brilliant daylight. Thus during winter, their depression tops.

5. Psychotic Depression

People experiencing psychotic depression have symptoms like depression alongside psychotic symptoms like visualizations, daydreams, neurosis, and so on.

6. Post pregnancy anxiety

This is the form of depression that involves ladies in the period following childbirth. This could happen because of the clearly overpowering experience, an abundance of thoughtfulness regarding the newly conceived, and so on.

The above-given types are the six most normal types of depression analyzed among people. While the effect and the treatment for these forms of depression may contrast, the symptoms are comparative for the vast majority of them. Recorded underneath are the most well-known symptoms.

Symptoms of Depression:

• Lack of appetite or overabundance of appetite.

• Lack of enthusiasm for exercises you once cherished doing.

• Sudden weight reduction or weight gain

• Sleeplessness (a sleeping disorder) or exorbitant rest

• Fatigue

• Reckless behavior

• Thoughts of death, suicide, and so forth.

• Self-despise or self-hatred

• Unexplained blame and anger

• Crying for reasons unknown, getting agitated effectively

Forms of depression

1. major depression
2. Dysthymia, mild chronic depression
3. Atypical depression

4. Postpartum depression
5. Seasonal depression (seasonal affective disorder)
6. Psychotic depression

Forms of depression

Major Or Clinical Depression

A constant feeling of hopelessness and despair is a sign that you may have major depression, also called clinical depression.

In the event of major depression, it can be difficult to work, study, sleep, eat, and enjoy friends and activities. Some people experience clinical depression only once in their lives, while others experience it many times in their lives.

strong depression can sometimes occur from one generation to another in families but can often affect people without a history of the disease.

Most people feel sad or weak at some point in their lives. But clinical depression is characterized by a depressed mood most of the day, sometimes often in the morning, and a loss of interest in normal activity and relationships: symptoms occur daily for at least two weeks. Additionally, according to DSM-5, a handbook used to diagnose mental health problems, you may have other symptoms with major depression. These symptoms may include:

Fatigue or loss of energy almost daily.

Feelings of worthlessness or guilt almost daily.

Decreased concentration, indecision.

Insomnia or hypersomnia (excessive sleep) almost daily.

Interest or pleasure decreases significantly in almost all activities almost daily (called anhedonia, this symptom may be indicated by reports from other significant people)

Shaking or sensation of deceleration

Recurring thoughts of death or suicide.

Major weight loss or gain(more than 5% change in body weight in a month)

People at risk of severe depression

According to the National Institute of Mental Health, major depression affects about 6.7% of the US population over the age of 18. Overall, between 20% and 25% of adults have had a major depression episode at some time in their lives.

Major depression also affects older adults, adolescents, and children but is often undiagnosed or treated in these populations.

Do women have a higher risk of major depression?

Almost twice as many women as men suffer from major or clinical depression; Hormonal changes during puberty, menstruation, pregnancy, abandonment, and menopause can increase the risk.

Other factors that increase the risk of clinical depression in biologically vulnerable women include increased stress at home or work, a balance between family and career, and caring for an elderly father. Raising a child will only increase the risk.

Signs of major depression in men.

Depression among men is not stated to be major. Men with clinical depression are less inclined to seek help or even to discuss all their knowledge.

Signals of depression in men may include irritability, anger, or drug dependence, and alcoholism (addiction may also be a source of depression rather than its result). Eliminating negative feelings can lead to outright violent behavior both inside and outside. It can also cause an increase in the number of illnesses, suicides, and homicides.

Factors causing main depression

Some common causes or triggers of major depression include:

Loss of a loved one after death, divorce, or separation.

Social isolation or feeling of deprivation

Major changes in life: movement, graduation, work change, Pension financial disputes with a significant other or higher person

Physical, sexual, or emotional violence

Diagnosis of major depression

A doctor like your GP or psychologist should conduct a proper medical examination. You may have a depression screening test during a regular doctor visit. The professional will ask you about your personal and family psychiatric history and ask you questions to help you identify the symptoms of major depression.

Blood tests, x-rays, or other laboratory tests cannot be used to diagnose major depression. Although, your doctor can conduct blood tests to help detect certain medical problems with depression-like symptoms. For instance, hypothyroidism can cause some of the same symptoms as depression, as well as abuse and use of alcohol or drugs, certain medications, and seizures.

How major depression is treated

Major or severe depression is a disease that is extreme but can be treated. Your family doctor or psychiatrist may recommend antidepressant treatment depending on the severity of the symptoms. It may also Consider psychotherapy or speech therapy to address the mental condition.

Sometimes other medications are put into the antidepressant to improve its effectiveness. Some drugs work best for some people. Your doctor may have tried different medications in different doses to determine which one is for you.

There are other therapeutic options for clinical depression, such as electroconvulsive therapy, also called ECT or shock therapy, which can be used if the medications are not effective or if the symptoms are severe.

Prevention of major depression

Once you have had one major depressive episode, You're at a high risk of another. The best approach to prevent another episode of depression is to find out the causes or causes of major depression (see above) and continue to take the prescribed medication to prevent a relapse. It is also important to know the symptoms of major depression and talk to your doctor first if you have any of these symptoms.

Dysthymia

Dysthymia sometimes called mild and chronic depression is less severe, and has fewer symptoms than major depression. With dysthymia, symptoms of depression can last a long time, often two years or more. People with dysthymia can also go through periods of major depression, sometimes referred to as' double depression.' Dysthymia and chronic depression are now known as "persistent depressive disorders" in modern diagnostic classification systems.

Causes of dysthymia

Doctors are unsure about the causes of depression or dysthymia. Genes may play a role, but many affected people do not have a family depression history, and others with a family history have no depression problems. Abnormal functioning in the circuits of the brain or the pathways of nerve cells that connect the various regions of the brain that regulate mood would also be involved. Major life stressors, chronic illnesses, medications, and even relationship or professional problems can also increase the risk of dysthymia in people biologically predisposed to the development of depression.

Dysthymia symptoms

Dysthymia symptoms are the same as major depression symptoms, but they are less frequent and less severe. They include the following:

Sadness or depression, almost all day or almost Loss of pleasure in things that were once pleasant.

Significant weight change (gain or loss of more than 5% of weight in a month) or appetite Insomnia or excessive sleep almost daily. Being physically agitated or decrepit in a way noticeable to others.

Fatigue or loss of energy almost daily. Feelings of hopelessness or uselessness or excessive guilt almost daily.

Problems concentrate or make the decision almost daily.

Recurring thoughts of death or suicide

Diagnosis Diagnosis Dysthymia

A mental health specialist usually diagnoses the symptoms of the person. In the case of dysthymia, these signs will last longer and will be less severe than in patients with major depression.

In the event of dysthymia, your doctor will want to make sure that the symptoms are not the result of a physical condition such as hypothyroidism.

If you are depressed and have depressive symptoms for more than two weeks, consult your doctor or psychiatrist. Your provider will perform a correct medical evaluation paying particular attention to your personal and family psychiatric history.

There are no blood tests, X-rays, or other laboratory tests that can be used to diagnose dysthymia.

Treatment for dysthymia

Dysthymia is a serious disease, But it can also be handled very well. In the case of any chronic illness, early diagnosis and medical treatment can reduce the intensity and length of symptoms, as well as the likelihood of a major depressive episode.

To treat dysthymia, physicians may use psychotherapy (dialogue therapy), medications such as antidepressants, or a combination of these therapies. Dysthymia can often be treated by a primary care physician.

Psychotherapy

Psychotherapy (or logotherapy) is used in the treatment of dysthymia and other mood disorders to help the person develop appropriate skills to deal with the difficulties of daily life and their opinions. False and wrong about yourself. Psychotherapy can also help increase medication adherence and healthy lifestyle habits and help the patient and family understand the mood disorder. You can take advantage of individual therapy, family therapy, group therapy, or a support group with others living with chronic depression.

Antidepressants Help to ease dysthymia

There are different classes of antidepressants that are available to treat dysthymia. Your doctor will determine your physical and mental health, including other health issues, and then find the most effective antidepressant with the least number of side effects.

It may take several weeks for antidepressants to work properly. They should be taken at least six to nine months after an episode of chronic depression. In addition, it may take several times a week to stop an antidepressant safely. Therefore, let your doctor guide you if you decide to discontinue treatment.

Sometimes, antidepressants have uncomfortable side effects. This is why you should work hand in hand with your doctor to locate the antidepressant that gives you the most benefit with the least side effects.

What can I do to feel better?

Obtaining an accurate diagnosis and effective treatment is an important step to feeling better about chronic depression. Also, consult with your doctor about the benefits of a healthy life, such as a balanced diet, regular exercise, prevention of alcohol and tobacco use, and strong social support between parents and family. Family Members These positive habits are also important for improving mood and well-being.

Can Dysthymia Worsen?

A person with dysthymia also experiences, at the same time, an important episode of depression. This is called double depression. Therefore, seeking an early and accurate medical diagnosis is so important. Afterward, your doctor may recommend the most effective treatment to help you feel this way.

Atypical depression

Atypical depression is a subtype of major depression or dysthymia with several specific symptoms., including an appetite or weight gain, drowsiness or excessive sleepiness, marked fatigue or weakness, mood highly responsive to environmental conditions, and extreme sensitivity. to refuse

What is atypical depression?

Atypical depression can be a "specifier" for major depression or dysthymic disorder. People with atypical depression had often faced depression from an early age when they were teenagers.

- A person with classic major depression has at least five of the following nine symptoms:
- Sadness or depression, almost all day or almost
- Loss of satisfaction in once pleasant things.
- Major weight change (gain or loss of more than 5% of weight in a month) or appetite
- Insomnia or excessive sleep almost daily.
- A state of physical agitation or decomposition noticeable to others.
- Fatigue or loss of energy almost daily.
- Feelings of hopelessness or uselessness or excessive guilt almost daily.
- Problems with concentration or decision almost daily.
- Recurring thoughts of death or suicide, a suicide attempt.

The dysthymic disorder, which is now known in the psychiatric community as major chronic depression or"persistent depressive disorder," is a condition that involves the presence of depressed mood longer than for at least two years in adults. . (one year in children and adolescents). adolescents) at least two of the above-associated symptoms, but less than the five symptoms that identify as the major depressive episode.

Despite its name, atypical depression is very known. It is contrasted with "melancholic" depression, another subtype of depression, which involves symptoms of insomnia (rather than getting too much sleep), loss of appetite (rather than increased appetite), a relative lack of response to the mood: environmental conditions and a significantly reduced ability to feel pleasure.

Treatment for atypical depression.

Doctors are likely to recommend psychotherapy and/or medication for atypical depression, depending on the severity of the symptoms. There are different types of psychotherapy and medication available for treatment. You may be referred to a specialist like a psychiatrist, psychologist, or other licensed mental health professional.

Mood reactivity is one of the main characteristics of atypical depression that separates it from melancholic depression. However, the person with atypical depression sees their mood as a way to improve if something goes positive. In melancholic depression, positive changes rarely result in a change of mood. In addition, diagnostic criteria use at least two of the following symptoms to accompany mood responsiveness:

- Too much sleep (hypersomnia)
- Increased appetite or weight gain.

Having a more intense reaction or greater sensitivity to rejection, which leads to problems in social and professional relationships.

Feeling heavy, paralyzed, or "driven."

A doctor will study the physical causes of these symptoms. This will include a physical exam and tests to look for a problem such as hypothyroidism. In cases of hypothyroidism, having low levels of thyroid hormone can cause symptoms such as depression and weight gain.

Postpartum depression (PPD)

Postpartum depression (PPD) is a complex mixture of physical, emotional, and behavioral changes that occur in a woman after childbirth. According to DSM-5, a manual used to diagnose mental disorders, PPD is a major form of depression that appears within four weeks after giving birth. A postpartum depression diagnosis is based not only on the delay between birth and onset but also on depression severity.

What is postpartum depression?

Postpartum depression is linked to the chemical, social and psychological changes involved in having a child. The term describes a series of physical and emotional changes that many new mothers suffer. The good news is that postpartum depression can be treated with medication and counseling.

Physiological changes include a rapid drop in post-birth hormones. There is still uncertainty about the relationship between this deterioration and depression. But estrogen and progesterone are known is that the levels of the female reproductive hormones increase tenfold during pregnancy. Then they fall apart after delivery. Three days after childbirth, the level of these hormones returns to the previous pregnancy.

In addition to these chemical changes, the social and psychological changes associated with motherhood increase the risk of depression.

Symptoms of postpartum depression

Postpartum depression symptoms are similar to those that usually occur after birth. They also include difficulty sleeping, changes in appetite, excessive fatigue, low libido, and frequent mood swings. However, these symptoms are also accompanied by other symptoms of major depression, which are not normal after birth and may involve depressed mood; loss of pleasure, feelings of worthlessness, hopelessness, and helplessness; thoughts of death or suicide or thoughts or injuries to someone else.

Factors Risk factors for postpartum depression

Several factors can increase the risk of postpartum depression, including:

- History of depression before pregnancy or during pregnancy.
- Age at the time of pregnancy: the younger you are, the greater the risk
- The ambivalence of pregnancy.
- Children: The more you have, the more likely you are to become depressed in a subsequent pregnancy.
- with a history of depression or premenstrual dysphoric disorder
- limited social support
- Live alone
- marital conflict

□ What is the frequency of postpartum depression?

Most new moms experience "melancholy" after giving birth. About one in ten women will develop a more severe and more severe depression after childbirth. About one in 1,000 women develop a more serious disease called postpartum psychosis.

Different types of postpartum depression

There are three types of mood relief in women after childbirth:

The child's melancholy, which occurs in most women a few days after the birth, is considered normal. A new mother is burnt with humor, like feeling very happy and then very sad. You can cry for nothing and feel impatient, irritable, agitated, anxious, alone, and sad. The baby's sadness can only last for a few hours, or even a week or two after giving birth. The sadness of the child does not generally require treatment from a medical provider. Often joins a new group of moms support or talk to other moms helps.

Postpartum depression (DPP) may occur a few days or months after delivery. SPP can occur after the birth of a child, not just the first child. A woman may have feelings similar to those of the child's sadness (sadness, despair, anxiety, irritability), but they feel much stronger than with the child's sadness. DPP often prevents a woman from doing the things she needs every day. When a woman's ability to function is impaired, she should consult her health care provider, such as her gynecologist or primary care physician. This doctor can detect symptoms of depression and develop a treatment plan. If a woman is not treated for PPD, the symptoms can be worse. Even though PPS is a serious disease, it can be treated with medication and advice.

Postpartum psychosis is the most dangerous mental illness that can affect new mothers. This disease can occur quickly, often in the first three months after delivery. Women may lose touch with reality, have auditory hallucinations (listen to things that don't really happen, like a speaker) and delusions (strongly believe in clearly irrational things). Visual hallucinations (see things that aren't) are less common. Other symptoms include insomnia (inability to sleep), feelings of anxiety and anger, rhythm, restlessness, and strange feelings and behaviors. Women that have postpartum psychosis need to be treated immediately and need medication almost always. Sometimes, women are admitted to the hospital because they run the risk of injury to themselves or another person.

How anxiety symptoms and obsessive-compulsive disorders affect postpartum depression

New symptoms of an obsessive-compulsive disorder rarely appear after postpartum (approximately 1% to 3% of women). Obsessions are usually related to the health of the child or irrational fears of harming the child. A panic disorder can occur. Both conditions often coexist with depression.

Tips for coping after childbirth

Here are some tips to help bring a newborn home:

- Ask for help: Tell others how they can help you.
- Be realistic about your expectations about yourself and the child.
- Exercise-to the extent of any restrictions your doctor may impose on your activity level. Go for a walk and let the house rest.
- Wait for the good and bad days.
- Follow a reasonable diet; Avoid alcohol and caffeine.
- Promote your relationship with your partner: Take time for others.
- Keep in touch with family and friends: do not isolate yourself.
- Limit the number of visitors when you first arrive home.
- Make phone calls.
- Sleep or rest when your baby is sleeping!

How is postpartum depression treated?

Postpartum depression is treated differently depending on the type and severity of the woman's symptoms. Treatment options include anti-anxiety or antidepressant medication, psychotherapy, and participation in a support group for emotional support and education. In severe cases, an intravenous infusion of a new medicine called brexanolone (Zulresso) may be prescribed.

Bipolar disorder

Then, bipolar disorder became known as manic depression. It is a type of major affective disorder, or mood disorder, defined by manic or hypomanic episodes (normal mood changes accompanied by high energy states). Bipolar disorder is a serious illness. Mania often involves insomnia, sometimes for days, accompanied by hallucinations, psychosis, delusions, or paranoid anger. To add to this, depressive episodes can be more devastating and more difficult to treat than people who have never had mania or hypomania.

Meaning of bipolar disorder

Bipolar disorder is a complex disorder that is probably the result of a combination of genetic and non-genetic factors. Related mood disorders include clinical depression or mania with periods of normal mood and moderate energy between episodes (extreme exhaustion and high energy). The severity of mood episodes can range from mild to extreme and can occur gradually or immediately over a period of days to weeks. When discrete episodes of mood occur four or more times a year, the process is called a rapid cycle. Rapid cycling should not be mixed with very frequent changes in mood that can occur in people with bipolar disorder or under other conditions like a borderline personality disorder.

In addition to manic or depressive episodes, patients with bipolar disorder may have thought disorders. They may also have perception distortions and an alteration in social functioning.

Causes of bipolar disorder.

As with other mood disorders, the causes of bipolar disorder are unknown. Bipolar disorder is known to involve dysregulation of brain function and sometimes has a genetic component (which can be exercised in a family).

At what age is bipolar disorder diagnosed?

Bipolar disorder is usually between the ages of 15 and 24 and persists throughout life. Short-term diagnosed mania is rarely seen in children or adults over 65 years of age.

The severity of symptoms varies among people with bipolar disorder. If some individuals have certain symptoms, others are at risk of working and living an ordinary life.

Marked by relapses and remissions, bipolar disorder has a high recurrence rate if left untreated. Patients with severe mania generally require hospitalization to protect against risky behaviors. Severely depressed people also need hospitality to prevent them from reacting to suicidal thoughts or psychotic symptoms (delusions, hallucinations, disorganized thoughts).

About 90% of people with type I bipolar disorder, which is the most severe form, have at least one psychiatric hospitalization. Two of three people had two or more hospitalizations in their lifetime.

Depression symptoms of bipolar disorder

The clinical symptoms of depression observed with bipolar disorder are the same as those observed in major depressive disorder and include:

- Not having an appetite and/or weight loss, or overeating and weight gain.
- Difficulty concentrating, remembering, and making decisions.
- Fatigue, loss of energy, "slowing down."
- Feelings of guilt, futility, helplessness.
- Feelings of despair and pessimism.
- Insomnia, morning noise, or excessive sleep
- Loss of interest or enjoyment for hobbies and activities that have been practiced once, including sex.
- Persistent physical symptoms that do not correspond to treatment, such as headache, digestive disorders, and chronic pain.
- persistent sad, anxious or "empty" mood
- agitation, irritability
- Death thoughts or you want to take your life, attempts of suicide.
- What are the symptoms of mania in bipolar disorder?
- Signs of mania in bipolar disorder include:
- Disconnected and very fast thoughts (in the race)
- great beliefs
- Inappropriate exaltation or euphoria.
- Inappropriate irritability
- inappropriate social behavior
- Increased sexual desire.
- Faster or volume of conversation.
- Considerable energy growth.
- Bad judgment
- The need for sleep was reduced due to high energy.

In the case of postpartum psychosis, medications are usually added to treat psychosis. Hospitalization is also often required.

If you are relieved, do not assume that you cannot take medication for depression, anxiety, or even psychosis. Talk to your doctor. Under the supervision of a doctor, many women take medication while breastfeeding. It's a decision you have to make between you and your doctor.

When should a new mother seek professional treatment?

Post-treatment depression cannot be harmful to new mothers and their children. A new mother should seek the help of a professional when:

- Symptoms persist for more than two weeks.
- She can't function normally.
- Can not cope with everyday situations.

bipolar II disorder

Although mania is the main feature of bipolar disorder I, bipolar disorder II has lower periods of exaltation, called hypomania. There are also episodes of major depression. According to the diagnostic manual published by the American Psychiatric Association, the DSM-5, the difference between hypomania and mania is "the degree of severity" and the absence of psychosis (delusions or hallucinations) in hypomania and without the negative impact of "high" symptoms in work and social functioning.

Signs of hypomania in bipolar II disorder

The signs of hypomania in bipolar II disorder include:

- Needs to sleep.
- Extreme focus on projects at home or at work.
- exuberant and exalted humor
- More secure
- Great creativity and productivity.
- Increased energy is at libido.
- reckless behavior
- risky pleasure in pursuing behaviors

How to diagnose bipolar disorder?

There is no experimental examination or brain imaging tool for diagnosing bipolar disorder; as with most mood disorders, your doctor will evaluate your signs and symptoms after a physical examination. Your doctor will also inquire about your medical history, both personal and family. Laboratory tests can be performed to exclude other disorders that may affect mood.

Therefore, your doctor may want to talk to family members about whether they can identify when you are exalted and overactive. Because exaltation may seem good or normal compared to depression, it is often difficult for someone with Bipolar disorder to know if their mood is too heavy. In ways that cause serious problems and shame, Mania often affects thinking, judgment, and social behavior. For example, when an individual is in a manic phase, business or financial decisions can be taken. Early diagnosis and effective treatment are, therefore, very important in bipolar disorder.

About 3% of Americans have bipolar disorder in their lifetime. Here are 18 famous people who have been diagnosed with bipolar disorder.

- [ ] **Treatment for bipolar disorder**

Bipolar disorder treatment may involve the use of mood stabilizers such as lithium. Some anticonvulsants, antipsychotics, and benzodiazepines may also be used to stabilize mood. Antidepressants are sometimes associated with mood stabilizers to stimulate depressed mood, although these antidepressants are often not as effective as some type of mood stabilizers or atypical antipsychotics for the treatment of depression in bipolar disorder.

Seasonal depression

Winter depresses you more than you think? However, you may have seasonal depression, also known as seasonal affective disorder (SAD).

Seasonal depression is a mood disorder that occurs every year at the same time. A rare form of seasonal depression called "summer depression" begins in late spring or early summer and ends in the fall. In general, however, the affective disorder of the season begins in the fall or winter and ends in spring or early summer.

Causes of seasonal depression.

The reason we do not know the exact causes of ASD, some scientists believe that some deep in the brain hormones cause mood changes related to certain times of the year. Experts believe that ASD could be linked to these hormonal changes. According to one theory, less sun in autumn and winter causes the brain to produce less serotonin, a chemical that is linked to the brain that regulates mood. When the pathways of nerve cells in the brain that regulate mood do not function normally, feelings of depression and symptoms of fatigue and weight can occur.

CAS usually begins in early adulthood and is more common in women than in men. Some people with ASD have mild symptoms and uncomfortable or irritable symptoms. Others have more severe symptoms that interfere with relationships and work.

Due to the lack of light during winter, it is less common in very sunny countries throughout the year.

Winter symptoms

People with SAD have several early signs of depression, including:

- Menu energy
- difficulty concentrating
- worn out
- stronger appetite
- A great desire to be alone.
- Need more sleep.
- weight gain
- summer symptoms
- less appetite
- Sleep disorders
- Weight loss
- diagnosis

If you are depressed and have any of the above symptoms, consult your doctor for an evaluation. He or she is going to recommend the right treatment for you.

Treatment of seasonal depression

Depending on the severity of your symptoms, different treatments are available. Furthermore, the medication may be different if you have another type of depression or bipolar disorder.

For seasonal depression, conventional antidepressants are often used. Bupropion XL is currently the only medication approved by the FDA specifically to prevent major episodes of depression for people with SAD.

Many doctors recommend that people with SAD leave early in the morning to get more natural light. If this is not possible due to the dark winter months, antidepressants, or light therapy (phototherapy) may be helpful.

Some researchers associate seasonal depression with the natural hormone melatonin, which causes drowsiness. Light affects the biological clock of our brain that regulates circadian rhythms, a physiological function that may include mood swings when there is less sun available in winter. Natural light or "full-spectrum" can have an antidepressant effect.

A full spectrum light illuminates your eyes indirectly. It sits about 2 meters away from bright light, approximately 20 times brighter than lighting in a normal room. The therapy begins with a session of 10 to 15 minutes a day. Then, the duration increases from 30 to 45 minutes daily, depending on your answer.

Do not look directly at the light source of a light box for long periods of time to avoid damaging the eyes.

Some people with SAT recover a few days after using light therapy. Others take a lot more. If the symptoms of SAD do not go away, your doctor may increase your phototherapy sessions twice a day.

People responding to light therapy are encouraged to continue until they can be in the sun again in the spring. Although the side effects are minimal, be careful if you have sensitive skin or a history of bipolar disorder.

Prevention

- Spend time outside every day, even on cloudy days. The effects of daylight always help.

- Start using a 10,000 lux softbox in the fall, even before you hear the effects of CAS winter.
- Adopt a healthy diet. This will help you get more energy, even if you want high starch and sugar foods.
- Exercise 30 minutes a day, five times a week.
- Be involved in your social circle and regular activities. Social support is very important.

When should I call my doctor?

If you feel depressed, tired, and irritable at the same time every year and these feelings seem to be seasonal in nature, You can write the APR form. Open up about your feelings with your doctor. Follow his advice on lifestyle and treatment changes.

Your doctor may recommend light therapy; ask if the company provides light boxes for patients with SAD. You can also rent

or buy a lightbox, but they are expensive, and health insurance companies do not generally cover it.

Psychotic depression

Psychotic depression is a major subtype of depression that occurs when a severe depressive illness includes a form of psychosis. Psychosis can be a hallucination (such as the voice of a voice telling you that you are not good or not worth it), illusions (such as intense feelings of worthlessness, failure, or having committed a sin), or another pause with reality. Psychotic depression affects about one in four people admitted to the hospital because of depression.

How does psychotic depression differ from main or non-psychotic clinical depression?

According to the National Institute of Mental Health, A psychotic person is broken down from reality. people who suffer from psychosis can easily hear "voices. "Or they may have strange and illogical ideas. For example, they may think that others may hear their thoughts or try to harm them. They may also think that they are possessed by the devil or that the police want them to commit a crime that they have not actually committed.

People with psychotic depression can be angry for no apparent reason. They can also spend a lot of time alone or in bed, sleep during the day, and stay awake at night. A person suffering from psychotic depression may neglect their appearance to not wash and not change. Or this person may be difficult to talk to. Perhaps it's just thinking about things that don't have meaning.

Psychosis is also found in individuals with other mental illnesses, such as depression. But those who suffer from psychotic depression generally have delusions or hallucinations that correspond to the problems of depression (such as futility or failure), while psychotic symptoms in schizophrenia are often strange or unlikely and have no obvious connection with mood. (for example, strangers follow

him for no other reason than to chastise him). People with psychotic depression may also feel humiliated or ashamed of their thoughts and try to soothe themselves. This makes this type of depression very difficult to diagnose.

But diagnosis is important. Their treatment is different from that of non-psychotic depression. In addition, one episode of psychotic depression increases the risk of bipolar disorder with recurrent episodes of psychotic depression, mania, and even suicide.

What are the symptoms of psychotic depression?

Common symptoms in patients with psychotic depression include:

- agitation
- anxiety
- constipation
- hypochondria
- insomnia
- intellectual disability
- physical immobility
- Delusions or hallucinations.

Treatment of psychotic depression.

Usually, the treatment of psychotic depression is given in a hospital. In this way, the patient is strictly controlled by mental health professionals. Various medications are used to stabilize a person's mood, including a combination of antidepressants and antipsychotics.

Anti-psychotic drugs affect neurotransmitters that allow communication. Our ability to perceive and organize information about the world around us is regulated between nerve cells in brain areas. A variety of antipsychotic or neuroleptic drugs are widely used today. These are risperidone, olanzapine, quetiapine, aripiprazole, cariprazine, and asenapine. Each medication has unique side effects, and its clinical efficacy profile may vary. However, these drugs are generally better tolerated than previous antipsychotics.

Is it also the treatment for psychotic depression?

The treatment of psychotic depression is very effective. People can recover, usually in a few months. But continuous medical monitoring may be necessary. If the drugs do not help to stop psychosis and depression, electroconvulsive therapy (ECT) is sometimes used. It is important that the patient works with the doctor to find the most effective and least undesirable medicines.

Since psychotic depression is very serious, the risk of suicide is also high.

THE PLACE OF FORGIVENESS IN THE CBT TREATMENT OF ANXIETY AND DEPRESSION

Meaning Of Forgiveness

Forgiveness means different things to different people. As a general rule, however, resentment and revenge should be abandoned.

The act that hurt or offended you could always be with you, but forgiveness can lessen your control and help you get rid of the control of the injured person. Forgiveness can also generate feelings of understanding, empathy, and compassion for the person hurting you.

Forgiveness does not mean forgiving or apologizing for the harm that has been caused or reconciling with the person who is the sole cause of the harm. Forgiveness brings a kind of peace that helps you to continue living.

However, outside the scientific community, many people are a little confused about this concept.

A common but wrong belief is that forgiveness means leaving the person who would make you safe. However, forgiveness is not the same as justice, and there is no need for reconciliation, says Worthington. A former victim of abuse should not reconcile with an aggressor who remains potentially dangerous, for example. But the victim can always reach an empathetic and understanding place. "Sorry or not, nothing will change if justice is done," says Worthington. "Forgiveness is in pain."

It caused the damage. Forgiveness brings a sort of peace that allows you to carry on.

Many people think that forgiveness is about letting go or passing. But there's more to it, says Bob Enright, Ph.D., a psychologist at the University of Wisconsin, Madison, who pioneered the study of forgiveness three decades ago. True forgiveness goes even further, he says, offering something positive (empathy, compassion, understanding) to the person hurting you. This element makes forgiveness a virtue and a powerful construct in positive psychology.

However, outside the scientific community, many people are a little confused about this concept.

A common but wrong belief is that forgiveness means leaving the person who would make you safe. However, forgiveness is not the same as justice, and there is no need for reconciliation, says Worthington. A former victim of abuse should not reconcile with an aggressor who remains potentially dangerous, for example. But the victim can always reach an empathetic and understanding place. "Sorry or not, nothing will change if justice is done," says Worthington. "Forgiveness is in pain."

Another common misconception is that forgiving someone is a sign of weakness. "At that, I say, well, the person shouldn't try," says Worthington.

And some very good reasons to make an effort may be there. Evidence has shown that forgiveness is associated with mental health problems, such as reducing anxiety, depression, and major psychiatric disorders, as well as increasing signs of physical health and lower mortality rates. In fact, researchers have gathered enough evidence of the benefits of forgiveness to fill a book. Toussaint, Worthington, and David R. Williams, Ph.D., have published a 2015 book, "Losing Health," detailing the physical and psychological benefits.

FORGIVENESS OF THE SELF

Forgiveness does not necessarily involve others. Throughout life, it may be necessary to forgive yourself for reprehensible, real, or perceived acts. Some people who make the decisions they later complain about may find it hard to forgive them for making the decisions. People also tend to be subjected to higher levels of responsibility than others, which is more difficult to forgive than to forgive another person who has committed a similar crime against them.

Research shows that those who forgive themselves easily after making mistakes may notice a decrease in their empathy and may be less inclined to change their partner. Forgiving yourself can be more effective and beneficial when it includes careful reflection on the error, admitting the error, empathy for the other side, and some kind of reparation for the crime.

Because seizing angry feelings or other negative emotions, even self-directed, can cause a decrease in emotional, mental, and physical well-being, it is important to forgive. However, it can take a long time. When you have trouble forgiving yourself, there can be problems such as anxiety, depression, and stress, which can also cause physical symptoms such as high blood pressure, pain, and fatigue or lead to self-care. People who hold a grudge against themselves may also be more likely to engage in risky and risky behaviors, such as alcohol or drug abuse.

TYPE OF FORGIVENESS

DECISION BASE ON FORGIVENESS

DiBlasio emphasizes voluntary decision and willingness to forgive:

Decision-based forgiveness is defined as the cognitive relinquishment of resentment, bitterness, and the need for revenge. However, this is not always the end of pain and emotional distress. Forgiveness is perceived here as an act of will, an option to leave or keep. Persons should distinguish from their feelings of misery, their thoughts of resentment and bitterness.

The model behind DiBalsio's decision is to renounce resentment and bitterness cognitively but does not take into account the feelings of suffering that often persist after the election.

Cognitive excuse

Another cognitive concept of forgiveness is based on the belief that transgressions are cognitive systemic breaches, such as beliefs, for example. A cognitive approach to forgiveness uses standard cognitive therapy and psychodynamic therapy interventions to help people modify their knowledge.

One example is the cognitive model that proposed a definition of forgiveness as follows:

"The framework of a perceived transgression as the responses to the transgressor, the transgression, and the consequences of the transgression are transformed from negative to neutral or positive. The source of the transgression, and therefore the object of forgiveness, maybe yourself, another person or persons, or a situation that is considered out of the control of any person, such as a disease, fate, or a natural disaster. "

Emotional Excuse

Worthington described true forgiveness as something that only occurs when emotional forgiveness will occur because it needs emotional replacement.

When emotional forgiveness is complete, the person has replaced negative emotions associated with impotence, such as anger, resentment, and revenge, with positive emotions such as empathy, compassion, sympathy, and sympathy. Love in altruism

They argue that, at the beginning and at the end, the change in emotional forgiveness will be more accurately reflected by changes in emotions, not changes in thoughts, motivations, or behavior, although these often also occur.

The process of forgiveness

Forgiveness is, first and foremost, a process. There is the intrapersonal process of letting go of anger, and Interpersonal forgiveness that involves the offender is not always necessary.

The trick is to understand that social forgiveness can be contingent and not always necessary. Conditional pardon is not a real pardon because true pardon is self-service; it is our internal operation.

The distinction between decision forgiveness with regard to the external process and emotional forgiveness in relation to internal abandonment is very important. Forgiveness does not work well when a person feels that it is not their choice to forgive, and forgiveness as an option is presented below.

Forgiveness has been described as a process of change by McCullough that suggests that what differentiates a focus from seeking the benefits of other approaches, such as seeking empathy or relational commitment, is one positive approach.

McCullough has shown that writing about the benefits of interpersonal transgressions can be an effective form of intervention until it allows for cognitive treatment that facilitates forgiveness:

When our participants described the real or potential benefits of their recent transgressions (a task they found remarkably easy to do), they found a reduction in reasons for avoiding generosity and discounts.

Revenge, a motivation that underlies forgiveness.

There are different approaches to the process of forgiveness, and perspective has been shown to be one of the most effective ways to practice forgiveness because it allows us to connect with the transgressor as a human. Several studies on effective communication and couples therapy support these assertions.

Marshall Rosenberg's approach to non-violent communication explains how defining the needs of the other party can be helpful in learning how to take the other party's point of view.

Similarly, John Gottman's method of communication emphasizes that both sides of the discussion are valid and that taking into account the point of view of the other can also help facilitate the process of emotional forgiveness.

The ability to forgive oneself or to the forces of the universe (fate or God) is also an important part of the cultivation of forgiveness.

The level of acceptance that a person is capable of plays a key role in the efficacy of the forgiveness process, especially since some studies show that some cases of forgiveness can involve pain.

A meta-analysis of Wade, Worthington, and Meyer identified three elements common to all effective forgiveness interventions, regardless of the intervention model or theory based on the methods:

using different methods to reduce forgiveness,

they promised to forgive, and

empathize or experience positive emotions directed toward one another as an antidote to forgiveness.

Finally, Webb and colleagues define the process of forgiveness as a coping mechanism that adopts mindfulness and involves disease reformulation and neutralization.

They explained that greater vigilance could allow the patient to recognize the tendency to forgive faster and more easily, allowing them to use forgiveness as a saving mechanism.

How can I access a state of forgiveness?

Forgiveness is a commitment to a personalized change process. To move from suffering to forgiveness, you can:

Recognize the importance of forgiveness and how it can improve your life

Identify what needs to be healed and what needs to be forgiven, and why

Remember to join a support group or see a counselor.

Recognize your emotions about mistakes made and how they affect your behavior and work to free them.

Choose to forgive the person who offended you.

Get away from your role as a victim and release the control and power of the offending person and the situation in your life.

Withdrawal of shields will no longer define your life as you were injured. You can also find compassion and understanding.

What if I can't forgive someone?

Forgiveness can be difficult, especially if the person who has hurt you does not admit wrong. Found:

The practice of empathy. Try to see the situation from thc other person's point of view.

Ask yourself why you behave like this. Maybe you would have reacted the same way if you were in the same situation.

.Write in a journal, pray or use guided meditation, or talk to someone you have found wise and compassionate, such as a spiritual leader, mental health provider, or healer, or loving friend.

You know that forgiveness is a process and that even small wounds can be re-examined and forgiveness over and over again.

PERFIVITY BENEFITS

Forgiveness generally benefits more than forgiveness; Those who can forgive someone who has harmed them can achieve significant results. Studies show that disability or lack of forgiveness can negatively affect mental health and well-being and often contribute to conditions such as depression and anxiety. The personal benefits of forgiveness can be great: they can include greater happiness, better health, and stronger relationships.

People who have been most sorry for others have been happier and less likely to experience the negative effects of stress on their health. They can often resolve conflicts more easily, repair damaged relationships with friends or colleagues, and experience higher levels of empathy and more positive feelings toward people in general. They may also be more immune to the infection than fat since studies have shown that people who have one are more likely to weaken their immune systems.

Abandoning the ranks and bitterness can leave room for better health and tranquility. Forgiveness can lead to:

- healthier relationships
- Improvement of mental health.
- Less anxiety, stress, and hostility.
- decrease blood pressure
- Menu symptoms of depression.
- a stronger immune system
- Improves heart health
- Improvement of self-esteem.

Are there any health benefits?

Forgiveness is an emotional and cognitive process is characterized by the release of anger. It has been shown that anger felt in other places has negative physical, emotional and cognitive consequences over time.

Worthington and Scherer tell us that impulsivity, when viewed as a negative emotional and cognitive construct, is a source of stress. This means that forgiveness can be used as a strategy for emotional coping and can contribute to overall health as such.

Anger and animosity are related to the inability to forgive. These, in turn, had adverse health effects, especially on cardiovascular disease. Forgiveness, meanwhile, was associated with empathy and compassion for positive emotions.

A growing group of health theorists, therapists, and practitioners have suggested that the ways in which people respond to an interpersonal crime can have a significant impact on their health.

He found that people who forgive have more satisfaction with life than others and less depression. Lastly, these studies also showed that more people who forgive are more likely to think and less involved in any kind of ruminations, including:

ruminative depression is a form of repetitive thinking experienced by depressed people,

parents, which is a critical way of thinking about oneself or others, and

Reflective thinking and contemplation of the roots of feelings.

According to research conducted by researchers at Hope College, reliving painful memories and maintaining resentment has a negative effect on the emotional well-being and physical health of those who choose to rest.

Indulgent responses to anger, guilt, and hostility, as other studies show, have contributed to the deterioration of health status, especially coronary heart disease.

Study participants who were asked to imagine they did not forgive a criminal had more negative feelings, such as anger and sadness, were more excited, and had less control. Physiological effects include high heart rate, maximum blood pressure, and activation of the sympathetic nervous system.

NEGATIVE THOUGHTS

"Whether you think you can or you think you can't, either way, you are right!" – Henry Ford Our thinking processes are necessary for endurance and for competing in a cutting edge world. Critical thinking enables us to take care of problems quickly and effectively. Creative thinking enables us to create unique, various, and elaborate thoughts and connections. But it's the uninvited negative thinking that clutters our minds and often depletes our enthusiasm forever.

What is healthy thinking?

Healthy thinking can teach you to comprehend what thoughts of yours—both helpful and not helpful—affect problems or feelings that trouble you. With practice, you can learn to utilize accurate thoughts that encourage you instead of negative thoughts that discourage you. If you stop negative thoughts, you might be increasingly ready to care for yourself and handle life's challenges. You will feel better. What's more, you might be increasingly ready to maintain a strategic distance from or cope with stress, anxiety, rest problems, unwanted weight addition, or depression. Healthy thinking additionally includes calming your mind and body. You can utilize at least one technique. These may include muscle relaxation, meditation, yoga, or guided imagery. Cognitive-behavioral therapy, additionally called CBT, is a therapy that is often used to assist people with thinking in a healthy way. It focuses on thought (cognitive) and action (behavioral). Numerous people work with a therapist or a counselor to learn CBT. But you likewise can practice healthy thinking alone.

How does CBT assist you with thinking in a healthy way?

CBT includes techniques that you can practice daily to make healthy thinking natural. For example, You may be upset about reviewing a work call. His supervisor praised his work. But you are depressed because she has had some criticisms. You might even think, "I miss nothing about my particular job," or "She makes fun of me. I have to be bad." If I focus only on the bad, it is a case of negative or distorted thinking, you can teach yourself to perceive thoughts negatively, and you may wonder how true or useful your thoughts were. What exactly did my supervisor say? Were there positive comments? "Why am I focusing on criticism? "You can learn to see the reckless things you say you can do to prevent yourself from noticing the positive aspects of your life and your work. With practice and time, you can learn to make completely accurate and useful statements. You could say," I did a lot of good work. This year and my supervisor noticed, he thought I could improve the field, so I'll think about some things I can do to strengthen in this area. "CBT combines several ways to help you change your mind: Learn to keep notes of irrational thoughts about yourself. Learn to stop your thoughts. Learn to replace negative thoughts with specific thoughts. You can learn to relax your mind and body. This can reduce stress, and you can learn to manage better. It can also reduce stress.

Numerous people experience their entire lives victimized by their negative thoughts. They feel they have no control of what thoughts take up residence in their minds—and more awful, they accept the "voices" in their minds that tell them the sky is falling. While the negative inclination is genuine, it isn't impenetrable to your efforts for change and mindfulness. Though it might feel natural to enable your mind to meander into stress and sadness, you've reinforced negative thinking by not challenging it and by accepting your thoughts as your identity. But you have the ability to recognize this tendency and change it by building the reframing habit. The first step is to notice your thought patterns and interrupt them before they get out of control. Here are six strategies you can use throughout your day to break the pattern and start taming your mind. Each of these strategies takes just a couple of moments to utilize.

Strategy #1. Be the Watcher

Start by becoming mindful of your thoughts. Separate your "self" from your thoughts, and just see what is going on in your mind. The trick here is to do this in an impartial manner where you're not making a decision about a particular thought. Just be conscious of yourself as a detached witness to your thoughts. This exercise can be done sporadically throughout the day or during a meditation session. Watching your thoughts rather than attaching to them debilitates the thoughts and the emotions they foster.

Strategy #2. Name That Thought

Another way to separate yourself from your thoughts is by mentally acknowledging that they are nothing more than thoughts—not your reality. For instance, in the event that you think, "I'll never get the entirety of this done," change the mental discourse to "I'm having the thought that I'll never get the entirety of this done." This reinforces the fact that you are not your thoughts.

Strategy #3. Just Say No

At the point when you catch yourself in mental circling or stress, essentially state, "STOP!" out boisterous (vocalizing reinforces the interruption), and afterward envision an overwhelming metal divider pummeling down in front of your runaway thoughts. Barrie sometimes imagines pushing negative thoughts into a profound gap or putting them into an inflatable that floats away.

Strategy #4. Try the Rubber Band Trick

Wear a rubber band on your wrist. At whatever point you see it, stop and notice your thoughts. If you are stuck in negative thinking, but the rubber band on the other wrist or gently pop it on your wrist. This physical action interrupts the progression of negative thoughts.

Strategy #5. Know Your Triggers

Often, overthinking and negativity are triggered by an individual, situation, or physical state. Focus on common stresses and anxieties you brood over. Is there anything that happens that sets these off in your mind? Provided that this is true, write down the triggers, so you're informed when they occur. This mindfulness can help prevent you from being trapped by negative thoughts.

Strategy #6. Distract Yourself

Break the cycle utilizing distraction. Accomplish something that will occupy your mind, so there's no space for negative thoughts. Inundate yourself in a project that includes focus and intellectual prowess. In case you're stuck in the car or waiting in line, experience the multiplication tables in your mind or try to remember a ballad.

Truthfully, you will always struggle with some amount of negative thinking. You can't overcome a great many long periods of evolutionary wiring through sheer self-discipline. As Dr. Russ Harris says, "Any search for a 'pain-free existence' is destined to disappointment." However, you can deal with the torment by being increasingly proactive in what you permit to stay in your thoughts. Interrupting cluttered thinking is just part of the process of retraining your cerebrum and learning to disassociate from negative thoughts. Your mind hates a vacuum, so you have to fill the void with constructive thought, so you don't careen back into old patterns. Here are four ways to do this:

#1. Challenge the Thought and Replace It

You may notice that a considerable lot of your thoughts are uncontrollably exaggerated. They are not the truth, or if nothing else, not every bit of relevant information. You might think, "I'm a loser; I can never do anything right." At the moment, you certainly feel like a loser, but in the event that you look at the thought, you recognize that it's not entirely truthful. You've done plenty of things well and have been successful on numerous occasions. Rather than permitting "win big or bust" thinking to have a free pass, challenge these negative thoughts at whatever point they occur. This basically means coming up with a concrete model that contradicts the thought by reminding yourself of a positive event or past "win." For instance, let's say you're a writer who receives a negative review on a recent book. Your first thought might be, "I'm a terrible writer—everybody hates what I write." However, if you take the time to take a gander at the 100 past positive reviews, then you'll recognize that the majority of your perusers love your content. Utilizing positive reminders might feel clumsy at first, but eventually, you'll train yourself to interrupt those cycles of negative thinking. This habit causes you to take control of your reality and puts a roadblock in front of the ceaseless highway of self-sabotaging beliefs.

#2 Practice Acceptance

One question you might have is, "what do you do about those negative thoughts that are true?" In other words, how would you cope in those times when there is a legitimate explanation behind having negative thoughts? The truth is that there are times when you'll feel like it's difficult to maintain a positive outlook. Nonetheless, it's likewise true that the thoughts and feelings about these challenging situations are often far more awful than the situation itself. You can't completely eradicate your troubled thoughts during tough times, but you can decrease them through acceptance. At the point when you struggle against the reality of a bad situation, you're adding another layer of enduring to your psyche. You can't worry or guilt yourself into a solution. Instead, you need a clear head and a calm mind. At the point when you find yourself struggling and ruminating, stop for a moment and essentially state, "I accept this situation is going on." Take a full breath and try to stop mentally fighting against it. As you accept this challenge, you can...

- Determine any actions to take to improve or rectify it.
- Seek out anything positive you can learn from it.
- Find ways to get support as you are suffering it.

Acceptance of a situation doesn't mean you stay away from the action. It means you don't indiscriminately fight and claw to escape. You put yourself in a state of mind that enables you to take correct and helpful action.

#3. Take Mindful Action

Overthinking is normally a pointless activity, so why not turn that vitality into structured thinking and afterward action? At the point when your thoughts are cluttered, accomplish something positive that will distract you from negative thoughts. Just about anything that requires some intellectual competence and focus will work, but we suggest you take mindful action, an action that focuses on your values, goals, or priorities. A quick way to do this is to define your goals, which is something we discuss in the next section. In fact, one of the first mindful actions you could take is to define your values and priorities for the next year. Some other thoughts that you might try include:

- Writing
- Practicing an instrument
- Constructing something by hand Painting or drawing
- Working on a complex problem
- Studying
- Memorizing something
- Practicing a speech

- Designing something from scratch

These activities require focus and some degree of mental challenge, which prevents you from falling back into irregular overthinking or worry.

#4. Set a Worry Timer

You can't completely bring an end to the worry habit. There will be times when you're overflowed with such incredible negative thoughts that no amount of self-talk or distraction works. But in any event, during these times, you don't need to fall headfirst into the quicksand of negative thinking. You can limit the amount of time you spend in your head, so you don't sink so far you can only, with significant effort, get out. Set a timer for 10 to 15 minutes and enable yourself to stress over whatever enters your mind. Get it hard and fast! Take this time to express the entirety of the bottled up feelings and thoughts. In fact, during your "worry time," you might even jot down your thoughts in a diary. Writing in longhand causes you to process your thoughts and can often prompt a creative solution to your problem. At the point when the timer goes off, get up and accomplish something distracting (as suggested in the past strategy) to assist you with tapering off of this worrying time. If you find one worry session isn't sufficient, plan for one promptly in the day and one later in the afternoon. At the point when you start to get back into your head in between sessions, remind yourself to hold off until the next one.

INEFFECTIVE WAYS PEOPLE TRY TO STOP NEGATIVE THINKING

People often try a wide range of ways to get free of their negative thoughts, including distractions, redirections, or 'suffocating theirs distresses' just to later mentally beat themselves in the mood for being still stuck in their negativity. It can feel like a genuine internal battle. These are common techniques that attempt to stop the thoughts and numb the torment in the short term, but they just make things more awful in the long haul. It does not solve the problem at its core. The research shows that struggling with, contending with, trying to overwhelm, or push away unhelpful thoughts just intensifies them and makes things more awful.

An in depth approach to conquering negative thought is discussed underneath:

KEY ONE: Recognize and STEP BACK FROM NEGATIVE THOUGHT PATTERNS

Sponsors of negative thinking also repeat unnecessary thoughts. Refrain from comrades who describe "negative" emotions (unwanted or unpleasant) like anxiety, depression, stress, fear, unworthiness, dishonesty, etc. Once we learn that he recorded and identified negative thinking patterns as they occurred, we can begin to cancel them. This procedure departed from a thought called "cognitive defusion." In cognitive defusion, we learn what is simply in our minds as simple thoughts. That's not reality. You see, when we are stuck in our thoughts (cognitive fusion), we tend to think incredibly, really. We trust them. We buy them both, and we buy them. We put them at stake. When we have not merged with our thoughts, when we can return to cognitive deficits, we do not take our thoughts too honestly.

We hold them lightly. We possibly listen to them in the event that we find them important or helpful. We certainly do not consider our thoughts to be 'the truth,' and we don't automatically obey them or play them out. We consider ourselves to be as simply bits of language that cross the thoughts. Mental events, maybe, that move through the mind constantly, just like the weather goes through the sky. We have a choice by the way we choose to react to them. The model I like to utilize often to illustrate the difference between cognitive fusion and cognitive defusion is this... envision awakening one day and peering out the window and seeing rain. It's conceivable that a thought might come into your head that says, "what a repulsive day." Presently is it true that the day is shocking?

But of course not, it's just rain. In any case, if you embrace the thought of "what a terrible day," in other words, if you are caught up in cognitive fusion (literally fused with thought), think about what you are likely to have. That's right, and you're probably having a terrible day! In other words, if you embrace the thought in this way, you can generate what we might call negativity. I will further teach you as a fundamental means how to easily and quickly create cognitive defusion (expose your thoughts). It is part of our evolutionary history. There's nothing wrong with you. Generally, we have minds that are constantly advancing in the search for problems and dangers, so most of us have minds prone to many negative thoughts.

The problem isn't that we have negative thoughts. The problem comes when we accept our thoughts are true. At the point when you are never again entangled in thoughts, they lose their hold on you and lose their capacity to generate unpleasant emotions. Let's return to the model above. Envision, you're lying in bed in the first part of the day, you glance out the window, and you notice that it's raining, and once again, the thought emerges "what a repulsive day." If you are not fused with the thought (you don't buy into it), then your experience would be this way. You're watching the rain falling, then you likewise watch the thought (as simply a mental event) "what a horrendous day" emerge and fall away just like the rain is falling... and since you don't take it genuinely or trust it, it generates no negativity, passes by easily and you're allowed to lay there loose and calm, getting a charge out of the pitter-patter of the rain on top of the roof. As you can see, the ability to recognize unhelpful thinking and step back from it is incredibly liberating! It can change the quality of your entire day and, in reality, your entire life.

It's important to have the option to recognize the sorts of unhelpful thinking styles that can emerge, so here are some other negative thinking patterns that are most common. Be on the lookout for them, and underneath, I'll give you what to do when they show up...

ANXIOUS THOUGHTS AND WORRY

"My life has been loaded with terrible misfortunes, most of which never happened." ~ Michel de Montaigne

Worry is the point at which the mind projects into an envisioned future and conjures up scenes and thoughts about what could turn out badly. Here it often creates 'what if' scenarios. Sometimes it takes the form of envisioning or expecting that bad things will occur or that nothing good will ever happen for you. You might fret about your relationship going downhill, your health deteriorating, your car stalling, or your career being destroyed—despite the fact that nothing has actually happened yet. You could spend time concentrating on the lack of your life and accept that nothing would be better for you. Stress-related to your financial future, the well-being of your children or your partner allows you to fall into this category.

SELF-BEATING AND CRITICISM

Do you have a harsh internal critic? It is reasonable to say that you are always trying to get yourself ready, mentally beating yourself up for not being sufficiently good yet? Is it true that you are on a perfect strategy? Another pattern of negative thought is to constantly criticize and 'self improve' because you're not good enough yet. He can be extremely hard on himself and focus on all his perceived shortcomings and shortcomings. Similarly, you can extend this critical habitat to other people in your life. This can be a cause of great tension in relationships. Negative self-thinking and self-criticism often result in a lack of confidence and a lack of confidence.

Others may feel completely weakened by feelings of unworthiness, depression, or even suicide. There is nothing wrong with having goals and expecting them to be in better shape or health, etc. - We can simply choose them because they are good for us or we want to stretch and grow. It's a completely different free space to do these things because we still don't feel enough. When the mind constantly concentrates on what is wrong with you (and in your life) and breaks down to what is going well, one can remain trapped in negativity.

REGRET AND GUILT

Ruminating on botches made in the past frequently makes sentiments of disrespect, blame, and antagonism. Sentiments of uselessness may emerge when you play over and over in your psyche, 'awful' decisions, or 'wrong' activities you believe you have made. There is not much basically' about just pondering past encounters. This is the way by which we can learn, develop, and develop as individuals. Pessimism emerges when you harp on a circumstance over and over with no real expectation to learn and develop, yet rather you are self-beating or wishing things were diverse as opposed to being tolerating of things as they appear to be.

PROBLEMS

Negative thoughts frequently turn around what's going on with your life. Your attention becomes focused on and misrepresents the implied negative parts of your life. Here your mind will regularly make light of what is going well. For model, you may have an extraordinary family, food to eat, and shield; however, your car slows down, and it's all that you can think about and focus on all through the whole week. You enable the circumstance with the car to rule your thinking, and negative feelings emerge subsequently.

All week you are baffled, enraged, and depressed in view of the car when your focus could be extended to what is going splendidly and what you're appreciative for. The truth is that the car has an issue. It is rarely again running and ought to be taken to the repairman. That is a direct reality. Ruminating persistently on the circumstance isn't valuable at all, and is another way we can get caught in negativity. If you have this propensity for bemoaning your bothers and problems, you may always feel baffled, fretful, depressed, and impassive. Exactly when you're so caught up in what's going on, you can't notice what's correct. Paying exceptional mind to and perceiving these normal negative thinking designs when they emerge will help you with observing when to utilize the devices underneath to work with them proficiently and break free from their hold.

KEY TWO: COMING TO YOUR SENSES

"Let us not recollect harshly or forward in fear, yet around in mindfulness." ~ James Thurber

Notice that many negative thoughts, for the most part, stream from two headings. The first is deciding not to proceed onward—potentially, you ruminate over mix-ups, problems, blame, and anything in your life that is turned out inadequately the way you confide in it should have gone. The second is agonizing over the future—fear of what might occur for yourself, others, or the planet. This may appear as worry about whether you will accomplish certain objectives or nervousness about the security of your accounts or connections. Or, on the other hand, perhaps you may stress over getting old. Whatever your specific negative thoughts are, notice that in order to partake in negative ideas designs, the mind needs to cast its focus generally into the past or future. Either that or we condemn and rationally name things right currently to be 'bad.' When lost in negative thinking, we tend to be so occupied with thoughts that we totally lose touch with what is really occurring in the present snapshots of our lives. We miss the little joys of living every day. The daylight on your skin, the flavor of the food we're eating, a real association with someone we love while they are talking.

Exactly when we're lost on our heads, we lose touch with our general environment... .and we lose touch with ourselves. To become logically present and prepared to step out of negative thinking, one astounding technique is to 'woken up.' To do this, essentially divert your attention out of the thoughts in your mind and carry your focus to your sense perceptions. Whether you're in your home, at the workplace, in the diversion focus, or on a metro, notice everything around you. Utilize your senses to their fullest. Don't get into a psychological trade about the things you see; simply think about what you're encountering at this time. Know about the sounds, the fragrances, the impression of the air on your skin, or the contact points with the seat underneath you. Be there totally at the time. This is a form of mindfulness practice (progressively about this beneath).

Research from Prof. Imprint Williams from Oxford University showed that when challenges emerge in life, countless of us tend to become involved with exorbitant unhelpful thinking. Sometimes individuals attempt to stop consistent unhelpful thinking, yet we don't have to attempt to stop our thoughts. An undeniably viable approach to encourage such inside upheaval, Prof. Williams instructs, is to focus on our direct material experience. This present there's essentially practically zero room left in our attention for such over the top thinking. Coming to our senses quiets the mind and grounds us in the present moment. Now, it isn't so much that we intend to live totally submerged in our senses continually. It's proper to think when it's useful, obviously. Be that as it may, we can utilize this familiarity with our senses to the ground and focus on more prominent mindfulness when we find ourselves caught up in negative thinking. It is entirely hard to be both profoundly present at the time in our senses and prop the negativity up! Give it a shot as a test and find out for yourself to see whether this is valid.

KEY THREE: REGULAR MINDFULNESS PRACTICE

At the center of every last, one of us is a space that knows profound harmony. As we grow up, we tend to get progressively increasingly drawn into the mind – our problems, our objectives, our desires, our sentiments of fear and needs. We tend to get so involved, caught up, and lose touch with this progressively profound sentiment of self... this unadulterated unconditioned awareness. It gets basic for us to get progressively drawn into negative thinking, the more we lose touch with ourselves thusly and lose our mind. Truth be told, research from Harvard University shows that a great many people are 'mind meandering' 47% of their day, and this is the foundation of what causes subjective combination (entrapment with thoughts). Imagine the sea. Sometimes the surface waves can be tumultuous, yet the profundities are unaffected, quiet, and serene.

Our minds have a comparable nature. There is an ideal stillness in every one of us. Just underneath our molding, thoughts, and habits, which can sometimes, in like manner, be tumultuous, there is a tranquil spot inside, and it is constantly open to us as a quiet refuge. Mindfulness is the act of waking up to that wellspring of fulfillment and harmony. It's waking up out of mind meandering (where we are lost in our minds, our old convictions, habits, responses, and thinking designs) with the objective that we can live intentionally. Through mindfulness, we manufacture our ability to live from that progressively profound mindfulness and tame the mind. Regular mindfulness reflection has been seemed to diminish pressure, gloom, and tension similarly to improving safe capacity: people who practice reflection report by and large degrees of fulfillment with life higher than others. Actually, analyst and therapist Matt Killingsworth found that what makes people most cheerful is all things considered totally present at the time and that the more our minds wander, the more despondent we become. There is such a lot of power in this clear practice.

KEY FOUR: HELPFUL QUESTIONS FOR UNHELPFUL THOUGHTS

A couple of sorts of negative thinking examples can be very 'clingy.' You may find that you attempt to 'name it to tame it' and return to your senses, yet the thoughts keep on having a grip on you. On the off chance that you find yourself in this situation, there are some further apparatuses you can use to unwind from your thoughts and change your focus. These are known as helpful questions for unhelpful thoughts. These are drawn from ACT (acknowledgment and responsibility therapy). You can utilize a bit of these question to rationally address negative thoughts and use others to change your focus. Here are a couple of questions you can demand that yourself help you with unwinding from the idea. You ask them, and a short time later, you can answer them in your mind. Regularly you would simply pick one of these at some arbitrary time.

- Is this thought in any capacity valuable or helpful?
- Is it true? (Can I absolutely realize that it's true)
- Is this just an old story that my mind is playing out of habit?
- Does this thought assist me with taking effective action?
- Is this, though, helpful, or is my mind just chattering on?

Then you can (mentally) pose these inquiries below to create a new focus and new possibilities. These questions will assist you in focusing on constructive thoughts and actions and help you effectively face your day-to-day challenges and move towards living an increasingly meaningful life. Once more, you may just utilization these at a time, but you could always try more than one too.

- What is the truth?
- My deepest truth?
- What would I truly like to feel or create in the situation?

- How can I move towards that? How can I make the best of this situation?
- Who would I be without this negative thought?
- What new story or thought can I focus on now?
- How can I see this in a different or new way?
- What can I be grateful for at this time?

With these amazing questions, you can change your focus from being stuck in negativity to being focused on what's going great. They will likewise assist you with taking constructive action and move towards living a progressively meaningful life. Constructive thinking allows you to be happy when things are going well and puts problems in perspective when times get tough so you can stay calm and clear-headed and deal with them in a practical, efficient way.

USING A THERAPIST

Choosing to see a therapist is often a difficult decision. It must overcome the stigma of looking at a "psychologist" and must accept the fact that it cannot cope with life without the participation of another person. You're not the only one. Many people choose to see a therapist for different reasons. Sometimes they have reached a difficult life point, and sometimes they have a serious mental illness. Fortunately, therapy around therapy is disappearing, and it is much easier to ask for help today. In this chapter, we will discuss why you might want to see a therapist, and we will walk you through the process of finding the right one.

Would it be a good idea for you to Seek Professional Help?

The information and exercises in this book can support numerous people. Working through the sections that most closely relate to the issues in your life might be sufficient for you to get back, progressing nicely in your life. For others, seeing a therapist makes more sense. You might find doing the exercises in the book make sense, but you need extra help—somebody to walk through the exercises with you to offer insight and support en route. You might decide you need a partner in your quest to feel better. Or then again, you might feel your problems are too huge to deal with alone.

A portion of the reasons you might decide to see a therapist:

- Your current problem is too extreme for you to work through alone. Your symptoms have lasted two months or longer and are interfering with your relationships, employment, cleanliness, or ability to get chores done. You might have times when you feel better, but your symptoms continue returning.
- You have tried self-improvement programs, such as this book, and have seen some improvement but aren't satisfied with your advancement.
- Your problems are interfering with cognitive tasks, such as concentration and memory.
- You are utilizing the exercises but find it difficult to apply the concepts to genuine situations. You concur with the principles

of CBT and complete the exercises, but you can't make the jump from doing the exercises at home and utilizing them in your day by day life.

- You have gained ground by utilizing this book but have hit a divider and can't get past where you are currently. You want to continue to feel better and don't realize how to do that.
- You need somebody to keep you on track. You find that you lose motivation while doing the exercises, and working with a therapist can assist you with staying on course and consider you accountable.
- You find that you are making some hard memories uncovering core beliefs, and settling further emotions.

While choosing a therapist, it is important to distinguish between the two types of therapy and decide which is best for you. The following gives the general characteristics of each type.

Psychodynamic Therapy

Psychodynamic therapy has been around for quite a while and is often effective. This form of therapy, additionally called talk therapy, is the type of therapy normally portrayed in TV shows and films. With this approach, the patient describes their problems while the therapist listens and poses inquiries. Your therapist searches for patterns and significant events in your past that contribute to your current difficulties, often digging into childhood experiences to find reasons for your thoughts, feelings, and behaviors.

A portion of the characteristics of psychodynamic therapy include the following:

- Sessions are unstructured.
- The patient sets the agenda for the session by talking about what is on their mind.
- There are no homework assignments.
- Therapy focuses on close to home history just like the present.
- Your relationship with your therapist is considered central to therapy.
- Treatment typically lasts six months or longer.
- You sometimes meet more than one time seven days.

Critics of psychodynamic therapy consider it to be time-consuming and costly. The object to an undefined length of treatment, with certain people continuing therapy for quite a long time. This type of therapy has benefits. It provides you with a sheltered environment where you can talk about your feelings and behaviors without the dread of judgment. It gives you a supportive individual to work with when sorting out problems in your life. Numerous people feel this type of therapy exceptionally helpful.

Cognitive Behavioral Therapy

As you have learned throughout this book, CBT focuses on specific problems and the present time. The theory behind CBT is that irrational and faulty perceptions fuel your emotional difficulties. While you might discuss your past, the principle goal is to discover problems and make corrections in your thinking processes. A portion of the characteristics of CBT include the following:

- Treatment duration is between 12 weeks and 6 months, with the normal course of treatment being four months.
- Sessions are structured or semi-structured with deviation when required.
- You receive homework assignments to work on skills in between sessions.
- You and the therapist collaborate to set an agenda for each session. At the beginning of therapy, the therapist takes a greater amount of an active job; in later sessions, you mostly set the agenda.
- In the beginning, sessions focus on the present.
- You investigate past experiences to determine your patterns of thinking and behaviors that connect to core beliefs.
- Your relationship with your therapist is considered important but not central to therapy. The relationship is considered collaborative and active.
- You are a client, not a patient. Treatment depends on goal-oriented and problem-understanding approaches.
- You practice new behaviors and work on challenging old thinking patterns.

Numerous studies have indicated that CBT is as effective, if not more in this way, than medication in treating depression and anxiety issues. It is a practical approach and provides you with skills for dealing with difficult situations. The goal of CBT is for you to learn skills and techniques and carry them throughout your life, becoming your own therapist once sessions have finished.

Altogether, for therapy to be effective, you have to trust and feel safe with your therapist. You should be comfortable so you can talk about your problems, experiences, and feelings. You additionally need to consider practical matters, such as whether the office location is easily accessible, costs, and scheduling availability. Finding the right therapist often takes time. There are various online directories to help as you continued looking for a therapist.

www.ingramcontent.com/pod-product-compliance
Lightning Source LLC
LaVergne TN
LVHW022110200926
848481LV00003B/1134
9798201806835